Kris Dhillon

The New
Curry Secret

KRIS DHILLON

THE NEW
CURRY SECRET

RIGHT WAY

Photography by Nicholas Christopher

Contents

1. INTRODUCTION

INDIA IS A land of stark contrasts and startling paradoxes, and a culture with the kind of complexity, mystique and intrigue that develops only with a long, eventful and, at times, colourful history.

Many historians believe that Indian history and its cuisine are as old as mankind itself, evolving over the ages under the influences of travellers and invaders from all corners of the world, and from the emergence of various religions, rulers and cultures internally.

Despite this, Indian cuisine has not lost its original identity. It has instead become richer and more diverse, while managing to retain the core principle that everything we eat should be pure and balanced. Onions, garlic, ginger and spices, integral to Indian cuisine, have proven health-giving properties. Cook your curries with healthy oils such as olive, sunflower and safflower, using ghee, butter and cream in moderation, and you will have a diet that is not only compatible with a healthy lifestyle but one that contributes to it.

Indian cuisine is wonderfully rich and varied. The regional variations reflect the historical influences, contrasting demographics, culture and ethnicity of this vast and exotic subcontinent. With a multitude of vibrant dishes flavoured with aromatic masalas (spice blends) and fresh fragrant herbs, it is not hard to understand why Indian food has become a firm favourite all over the Western world.

Traditional Indian cuisine is split into four categories: North Indian, South Indian, East Indian and West Indian. However, ask for a Chicken Tikka Masala anywhere in India, and it is likely that all you will get is a blank look. 'Going out for a curry' is not an Indian pastime but in the West, and Britain in particular, it is a ritual that many people relish with gusto. Chicken Tikka Masala is reportedly the most frequently consumed dish in Britain and is even more popular than Fish and Chips.

The cuisine of Indian restaurants, loved by millions, does not fit into any of the traditional Indian cuisine categories, but it embraces some aspect of each, becoming in itself quite unique. It is this cuisine that holds the uncompromising, tantalizing allure for the vast majority of curry lovers in the West. The traditional recipes, as wonderful as they are, simply don't 'have it' when your tastebuds are crying out for the distinct, deep 'curryish' flavour and aroma of restaurant curries.

Indian restaurant cuisine has its origins in the period of the British Raj. Indian cooks, pressed by their British masters to prepare meals that were more acceptable to the British palate, modified traditional dishes for which the British rapidly acquired a taste. So much so, that the first Indian restaurants were opened in the affluent parts of London so that British officers returning home from their duties in India were not deprived of their favourite foods. This was the beginning of a new cuisine.

The second phase in the evolution of this new cuisine took place in the mid-1900s as families from Bangladesh, migrating to England to make their fortune, opened Indian restaurants in the East End of London, an area still famous for this cuisine.

A number of Anglicized Indian dishes were created during that early period, including the well known and loved Chicken Tikka Masala. Later in the century there was a rapid proliferation of Balti houses serving delicately spiced curries, freshly cooked in a wok-like pan. Beginning in Birmingham this new phenomenon rapidly spread to other parts of the country. The Balti dishes served in Indian restaurants are descendants of this cooking style and remain popular to this day.

There are now more than 9,000 Indian restaurants in Britain, employing over 70,000 people dedicated to satisfying an ever growing desire for Indian food.

In fact, Indian restaurant food has continued to grow in popularity all over the world. The Immigration Act of 1965 saw an influx of Asian immigration to the United States and with it an insurgence of Indian restaurants, especially in San Francisco, Los Angeles, Houston, Chicago and New York. All-you-can-eat buffets with an array of standard dishes are common in many Indian restaurants in the United States, catering for a growing appetite for Indian food amongst the locals.

Indian restaurants are also common throughout Canada, particularly in Toronto and Vancouver where large numbers of Indian nationals have settled since 1970. The cuisine of South Africa too boasts several dishes of Indian-origin; some have evolved over time to become unique to South Africa while many others are recognizably traditional Indian preparations modified with local spices.

In Australia the popularity of Indian food has increased considerably in the last 20 years, resulting in a rapid growth in the availability of Indian food and ingredients. Nearly all Australian towns and cities now enjoy the existence of several good Indian restaurants and eateries, and more are opening each month.

Until the publication of my book *The Curry Secret* in 1989, Indian restaurant cooking was a closely guarded secret of Indian chefs and restaurant proprietors. In *The Curry Secret* I told all and provided an easy, step-by-step guide, with all the little tricks of the trade to making Indian restaurant curries in your own kitchen – and the response was incredible. For the first time ever, anyone could reproduce their favourite dishes at home whenever they wanted to, and people loved it.

The Curry Secret remains in demand 20 years on. Nevertheless, the Western palate has noticeably changed and evolved over that time. There has emerged an avid and enthusiastic demand for dishes which challenge the modern Western palate rather than pander to the tastes of yesteryear when recipes were adapted to create milder dishes like Chicken Korma and Chicken Tikka Masala that were gentler on the tastebuds. Indian food is now integral to the British diet and restaurateurs have responded by creating more authentic dishes with a 'no-holds barred' approach to the use of more pungent spices and herbs.

There has also been a period of culinary evolution around the globe with a growing homogenization or mixing of cooking styles and techniques. Worldwide, professional chefs have sought to develop and promote the intermingling of a variety of popular cuisines, resulting in what has become widely known as 'fusion' food. Indian chefs too have embraced these developments and Indian spring rolls, Dhal Soup and Murgh (chicken) Ceylon are now commonplace on the Indian restaurant menu. While the favourites of the past decades remain popular, these elements of change have seen many more inventive restaurateurs create new and vibrant dishes.

In this book I seek to provide to curry lovers the know-how for creating these new and exquisite restaurant dishes, many of which had not yet been developed when I first revealed all in *The Curry Secret*. *The New Curry Secret* will show you how you can create the delicious restaurant curries of today, simply and easily. I have included all the closely held secrets, the special spice blends and tricks of the trade employed by Indian chefs plus some labour-saving tips and ideas to make it even easier when cooking Indian restaurant food at home.

If you own a copy of *The Curry Secret*, you will find that *The New Curry Secret* helps you take your cooking to the next level. Not only does it give you a plethora of delicious new recipes and cooking ideas, it goes a step further. It shows you what makes a good cook great; how you can transform good dishes into mouthwatering delights that are a feast for the senses, just by using a few simple techniques.

If you don't have a copy of *The Curry Secret*, you will discover for the first time the closely guarded secrets of Indian chefs. You will be surprised, delighted and amazed to learn how you too can easily produce delicious restaurant curries at home; curries that are as good if not better than the ones you enjoy in your favourite Indian restaurant.

THE 'NO SMELL' CURRY SAUCE

It is the curry sauce that, more than anything else, influences the flavour, appearance and texture of the typical restaurant curry and differentiates it from the traditional home-made one. It is also the curry sauce that enables you to cook one or more fabulous restaurant curries in next to no time. Have a quantity of this sauce on hand and you can put together an array of delicious, authentic restaurant curries in a matter of minutes.

However, there is no such thing as a free lunch – the smell of the boiling onions drives everyone out of the house for hours!

Well, not any more! The new curry sauce will have them staying right where they are; it actually smells good while it's cooking.

By making a few changes to the way the curry sauce is made, the unpleasant smell that emanated from the saucepan during the boiling stage has been eliminated. Furthermore, the new sauce is every bit as good as the original *Curry Secret* curry sauce. If you don't like the smell when making the curry sauce as outlined in *The Curry Secret*, you will love the new recipe.

Kris Dhillon

2. WHAT MAKES A GOOD COOK GREAT?

W HAT IS IT that makes a good cook great? What enables some cooks to take an ordinary, everyday dish and lift it to another dimension? The answer, as to most seemingly difficult questions, is a simple one – the best and the freshest ingredients available, and a passion for food.

Many people believe that poor quality meat and stale vegetables can be disguised by 'putting them in a curry'. This is completely inaccurate. A good Indian dish is a balance of spicy flavours around fresh, tasty vegetables and good quality meat or fish. No amount of sugar and spice can disguise tasteless, stale or out-of-season ingredients.

I'm not sure what kindled my own passion for food, but, whatever it was, it saw me standing on a stool so that I could reach the stove at the tender age of seven to make my first chapatti – under the watchful eye of my mother of course.

My family moved from India to England in the late 1950s when I was just five, and food always played an important part in our lives. It was difficult to buy many of the exotic ingredients that are so readily available today, so my parents grew whatever they could in the back garden. Meat was somewhat scarce and expensive in the years after the Second World War and, even though it was eaten only once or twice a week, it was common for those early migrants to buy cheaper, tougher cuts of meat and broiling chickens, and they developed inventive and clever methods of cooking them.

With my emerging interest in food and cooking I loved to watch my father cook the weekly meat curry. He would throw pieces of mutton, cheaper cuts of pork or portions of broiling chicken into a large aluminium pot together with a quantity of chopped onions and some salt. The pot was placed on a gentle heat and cooked slowly for up to three hours until the onions had melted and the meat was beautifully tender. He would then add generous amounts of ghee (clarified butter), ripe tomatoes, garlic, ginger, turmeric and freshly ground spices (which my mother had painstakingly ground to a fine powder with a pestle and mortar) until the colourless simmering mass was a fragrant, rich, golden red.

Just as you thought it couldn't get any better, in would go the spring onions plucked straight from the garden. Fresh green fenugreek leaves, again picked just before using, were roughly chopped and stirred in. Occasionally, if they were growing in the garden, my father would add sliced turnips or carrots or even spinach leaves, harvested at the last minute of course, and simmer them with the meat during the last hour or so of cooking. Finally, a generous sprinkling of freshly picked coriander would complete the culinary exercise. The aromas made your mouth water.

The fresh, aromatic vibrancy of those last few ingredients added so much to the character, flavour and appearance of these dishes, that they were transformed from being just good to being absolutely sublime.

My growing passion was further kindled when my mother decided to take me back to India for the first time since I had left the country some 12 years earlier. Expecting to be bored with and alienated by a country I had little memory of and possibly little in common with, I instead landed in a place that so fascinated me I tingled with excitement. The land that my parents farmed before they left for England had been well looked after and traditionally (organically) farmed by our extended family. The fields were full of corn, sugar cane, spinach, mustard greens, chillies, radishes, turnips, carrots, marrows, aubergines, spring onions, garlic and herbs and edible, exotic plants that I had never seen or heard of before. The people were different too: solid, pragmatic, salt-of-the-earth type individuals who were clearly in harmony with their environment and all its inhabitants.

Mealtimes were an absolute delight. My young cousins and I would rise early in the morning to make the short journey to the fields to pick the vegetables – aubergines, courgettes (zucchini), tender green chickpeas, turnips or carrots, chillies – and herbs for making breakfast, the meal consisting of a vegetable bhaji or dhal, buttery parathas, yogurt that had been made overnight, home-made green mango or lime achar (pickle) and lassi (buttermilk – a light fresh-tasting liquid that remains after yogurt is churned to make butter, done early each morning). Chai, flavoured with cardamom and made with fresh buffalo milk obtained that morning and sweetened with rich, sweet raw cane sugar (jaggery), followed shortly after.

When lunch and dinner time came around, the vegetables and herbs collected earlier were 'stale'. 'Feed them to the cattle,' my aunt would say, 'and go pick some more'. A few hours old, and they were no longer considered fresh enough for human consumption. Leftover yogurt from the day before was no longer eaten with meals as a side dish, but soured and thickened with besan (chickpea flour), flavoured with green fenugreek, whole spices, coriander and lots of fresh green chillies and made into a delicious curry. Any milk left over from the previous day was not fresh enough to drink and was either made into dessert using rice, sago, or vermicelli, or curdled and made into panir for cooking with ginger, garlic, tomatoes, chillies and peas to make Mattar Panir. Vegetables were so fresh that you didn't need to add water to make a sauce, their juices were copious enough.

Yet there was still more to come; I was fortunate enough to be in India at the time of the year that sugar cane is harvested and milled to squeeze out the juice. What a wonderful experience. I would eagerly arise at the chilly crack of dawn and make my way down to the mill, jug in hand. I had only a little memory of drinking freshly squeezed sugar cane juice (*ras*) and what a heavenly delight it was when I tasted it again for the first time. The cool, fresh sweetness of it was extraordinary.

These experiences were a revelation to me of how good food should be, but there is one particular incident that somehow transcended all of this and crystallized for me the sheer essence of fresh food. I loved to walk barefoot through the cool channels of water as they irrigated the fields, taking in this pure, bountiful countryside that they call the Punjab. During one such excursion, I leaned over and pulled a carrot out of the ground, shook it around in the water to wash off the soil and bit into it. The depth of flavour, the freshness of the aroma, the sweet, juicy 'carroty' taste were so pure and intense, it made me stop in my tracks and savour its stunning uniqueness. I had never tasted such true flavour before. It's as though my tastebuds came truly alive only at this moment. This experience made such an impression on me that I have recounted it many times. It was only a carrot, but I had never tasted anything like it, and the experience has shaped my relationship with food to this day.

The days were filled with delightful, mouthwatering episodes at every turn, beginning early with a long, cool, delicious glass of ras and ending quite late with fresh cobs of corn roasted in the embers of a dying fire followed by a glass of warm milk sweetened with raw cane sugar. I thought this must be paradise. I took great delight in learning to make new and complex dishes from my grandmother and aunts who were wonderful and creative cooks.

I became enthralled and enchanted by this mystical land, its people and the rich and sustainable lives they lived. They used no chemicals or foreign substances on the land. They looked after their animals, feeding them wholesome crops, linseeds and herbs. They used and re-used everything. The remnants of harvested corn and milled sugar cane were fed to the cattle or used as compost. Cattle and buffalo manure was used on the land or made into patties, dried and used as fuel for cooking and heating. Even the ashes that remained after the patties were burned were used for scouring pots and pans. There was no packaging, no waste and no landfill. Practices the West thought of as primitive then are now, with our awareness of climate change, environmentally friendly and ecologically sound.

I reluctantly returned to England after several months, but the essence of this magical country lives inside me to this day.

Tips on buying and using fresh ingredients

If you want to cook great Indian food, it is important that you obtain fresh, top quality ingredients, preferably organically produced. Just as you cannot make a silk purse out of a sow's ear, you cannot create a culinary masterpiece from stale, tasteless produce.

■ Buy seasonal fruit and vegetables. It is possible nowadays to buy just about every type of fruit and vegetable at any time of the year but at what cost to your tastebuds and your purse? Out-of-season fruit is generally tasteless and vegetables are bland and sometimes even bitter. Produce that is in season will taste a lot better and cost significantly less.

■ Buy local produce. Local markets and farmers' markets are good places to buy seasonal, fresh produce. You will be helping to save the planet too as the food has not travelled so far.

■ Buy the more exotic ingredients from Indian grocers. You will find the quality is top notch and the prices are lower.

■ When buying fruit and vegetables, pick them up, examine them and smell them. If they are fresh, they should be plump with smooth skins, feel heavy for their size and have a distinct aroma. Bunches of herbs should not be tired and wilting.

■ Buy organically grown produce when you can or grow some of your own. The appearance, feel and scent of really fresh produce, especially fresh herbs, are truly wonderful.

A little goes a long way to adding that touch of magic to your dishes. Try some of the following:

■ Homegrown coriander, for example, is so much more vibrant and aromatic than anything you can buy. Just a little sprinkled on the dish transforms it into something special, and you can grow it in a tiny area of your garden or even in a pot. During the warmer months, just sprinkle some coriander seeds from your pantry onto the garden or onto some potting mix in a pot, sprinkle some soil or potting mix on top, water and keep moist. It's that easy. Fresh coriander is a delicate herb. Use it towards the end of cooking and as a garnish.

■ Next time you have some garlic cloves or onions that are beginning to sprout, plant them in the garden. They will grow healthy green shoots in no time. Use the green tops, roughly chopped, next time you make a curry or savoury snack, and you will add an extra dimension of flavour, colour and aroma to the dish. Both of these ingredients need to be cooked so use them at the beginning of making a dish. (Note: much of the garlic available nowadays is imported and treated with a gas that effectively kills it, so it will not sprout. Buy organic garlic bulbs if you wish to sprout it and it will grow beautifully.)

■ Throw some fenugreek seeds (again the same fenugreek seeds you use for cooking) onto a small area in the garden, or into a pot and within a couple of weeks you will have fresh, green fenugreek leaves. Add a handful, chopped, to curries, bhajis, pakoras or really just about any savoury dish to impart a moreish, robust flavour to the dish. Fresh fenugreek requires cooking, so use it at the beginning.

■ A few fresh mint leaves shredded and sprinkled onto a salad, stirred into yogurt or even a curry add liveliness, colour and flavour. Mint grows easily and is a perennial. Ask a friend who has some growing in the garden to pull out a few roots and put them into a pot or straight into your garden. You will have fresh mint from late spring to early winter every year.

■ If you have a handful of sweet ripe cherry tomatoes, stir them whole or sliced in half into the dish at the last minute and you will introduce additional colour, texture and taste. The appearance of the dish is beautifully enhanced. Remember you feast with your eyes before your mouth.

Throughout the book, I have included suggestions for the use of one or more optional ingredients such as those above, and given instructions on how best to use them in your cooking. Please remember, though, you can make perfectly good dishes by following the basic recipes; these suggestions are an optional extra for those times when you are in the mood to create something extraordinary.

3. WHAT'S IN SEASON?

THERE ARE many good reasons why we should eat food that is produced locally and in season:

■ Locally sourced, in-season food is fresher, tastier, more nutritious and less expensive.

■ Due to the fewer 'food miles' that local produce travels, there is a lower consumption of energy and therefore less CO_2 emission.

■ The more you buy locally, the more you support your local community.

Clearly not all fruit and vegetables can be grown in all climates, and when local produce is scarce it is better to source food from neighbouring countries rather than those on the other side of the planet. The following list is a brief guide of what is best each season:

WINTER
Vegetables – Beetroot, Brussels sprouts, cauliflowers, Jerusalem artichokes, kale, leeks, parsnips, maincrop potatoes, pumpkins, rhubarb, swedes, turnips
Fruit – Apples, bananas, clementines, cranberries, kiwi fruit, lemons, oranges, blood oranges, pears, pineapples, satsumas

SPRING
Vegetables – Asparagus, aubergines, broccoli, purple sprouting broccoli, carrots, cauliflowers, leeks, new potatoes, radishes, spinach, spring greens, spring onions
Fruit – Apples, bananas, kiwi fruit, lemons, oranges, blood oranges, pomegranates

SUMMER
Vegetables – Aubergines, broad beans, runner beans, beetroot, carrots, courgettes, cucumbers, fennel, garlic, marrow, okra, onions, peas, peppers, early potatoes, maincrop potatoes, radishes, spring onions, sweetcorn
Fruit – Apricots, blackberries, blueberries, cherries, damsons, gooseberries, grapes, greengages, kiwi fruit, loganberries, mangoes, melons, peaches, raspberries, strawberries, tomatoes

AUTUMN
Vegetables – Aubergines, beetroot, broccoli, butternut squash, carrots, celery, courgettes, garlic, marrow, wild mushrooms, onions, parsnips, peppers, maincrop potatoes, swedes, sweetcorn, turnips
Fruit – Apples, blackberries, clementines, damsons, elderberries, figs, grapes, melons, nectarines, peaches, pears, pineapples, plums, quince, satsumas

4.

Every region of India brings its own unique influence and subtle variations to the popular dishes you enjoy in your favourite Indian restaurants. Spices that are fragrant, pungent, sharp, piquant, earthy and warm, and expertly blended are the essence of Indian cuisine. It is said that the flavours are as varied as the climate of India and as exotic as the people.

HINDI/PUNJABI	ENGLISH	HINDI/PUNJABI	ENGLISH
Achar	Pickle – sour	Gajar	Carrot
Adrak	Ginger	Garam Masala	Spice mix
Aloo	Potato	Ghee	Clarified butter
Amb	Mango	Gobhi	Cauliflower
Balti*	Karahi dish	Haldi	Turmeric
Bengan/Brinjal	Aubergine, egg plant	Hari dal	Green mung beans
Bhaji	Vegetable	Hing	Asafoetida
Bhindi	Okra (ladies' fingers)	Imli	Tamarind
Chai	Tea	Jaggery/Goor	Raw cane sugar/molasses
Chana	Chickpeas	Jaifal	Nutmeg
Chatani	Chutney or pickle	Jangli Dalchini	Cassia bark/
Chawal	Rice		Chinese cinnamon
Dahi	Yogurt	Jeera/Zeera	Cumin
Dalchini	Cinnamon	Jinga	Prawns
Dhal	Pulses	Kali Elaichi	Black cardamom
Dhanya	Coriander	Kali Mirch	Pepper
Dudh	Milk	Kalonjii	Onion seeds
Elaichi	Cardamom	Karahi	Wok-like utensil or
Faal	Fruit		serving dish

*In Hindi and Punjabi *balti* actually means 'bucket'. The word has taken on a new meaning within the context of the restaurant menu.

Hindi/Punjabi	English	Hindi/Punjabi	English
Keema	Minced meat	Piaz	Onions
Kela	Banana	Pootna	Mint
Kesar	Saffron	Raai	Mustard seed
Kulfi	Ice-cream made with condensed milk	Raita	Spiced vegetable yogurt
		Rajma	Red kidney beans
Kumbh/Khumba	Mushroom/mushrooms	Ras	Juice
Lasan	Garlic	Roti	Chapatti
Lassi	Yogurt drink	Saag	Puréed spinach and green leafy vegetables
Lowng	Cloves		
Machli	Fish	Sabji	Vegetables
Maki	Corn	Sakara/Kand	Sugar
Malai	Cream	Sarson/Saron	Mustard greens
Marss	Meat	Saunf	Fennel
Masala	Blend of spices	Shev	Apple
Masoor	Lentils	Shorba	Soup, gravy
Mattar	Peas	Suwa	Dill
Methi	Fenugreek	Takrai	Lemon grass
Mirch	Chillies, pepper	Tamatar	Tomato
Murghi	Chicken	Tandoor	Clay oven
Namak/Loorn	Salt	Tava	Hot plate for cooking
Nariyal	Coconut	Tej Patta	Bay leaf
Nimbu	Lemon	Til	Sesame seed
Paani	Water	Tulsi	Basil
Palak	Spinach	Tur (toovar)	Pigeon-peas
Panir	Cheese	Zafrani	Saffron

5. GETTING STARTED

S PICES are integral to Indian food. They add warmth, pungency, heat and the distinct aroma and flavour of Indian dishes. Creative chefs may use a dozen or more spices in one dish, but most cooks will do fine with a quantity of garam masala and one or two additional ingredients. You may want to keep other spices handy for particular dishes.

ESSENTIAL SPICES AND HERBS
Essential ingredients
- Green cardamom pods
- Black cardamom pods
- Coriander seeds
- Black peppercorns
- Cinnamon
- Cumin seeds
- Cloves
- Nutmeg
- Bay leaves
- Mustard seeds
- Turmeric powder
- Chilli powder

You will require the first nine ingredients in the list above to make garam masala.

Other useful ingredients
- Fennel seeds
- Fenugreek seeds
- Paprika
- Onion seeds
- Green mango powder (ambchoor)
- Tamarind
- Dried fenugreek leaves (methi)
- Jwain (carom seeds)
- Chat masala

Buying and storing spices: Spices are at their best when used within three months or so of purchase. Buy spices from an Indian grocer rather than a supermarket. Prices will be lower and the quality a lot better. To ensure maximum freshness and taste, buy whole spices rather than powders, and grind only in quantities that are likely to be used up within three or four weeks.

Store spices in glass, stainless steel or ceramic containers with tightly fitting lids, in a cool, dark and dry place.

How to make yogurt

Bring a litre (35 fl oz/2.1 US pints) of organic milk to the boil and cool until warm. Transfer the milk to a bowl or other container with a lid and stir in 2 tablespoonfuls of live plain yogurt. Wrap the container in a tea-towel and place in a warm place for 4–5 hours until set. Refrigerate.

How to make panir

Bring 2 litres (70 fl oz/4.2 US pints) of organic milk to the boil, turn down the heat and stir in the juice of a lemon. Continue to stir until the milk solids separate from the whey – add a few drops of vinegar if it doesn't completely separate. Strain the milk through a colander lined with muslin. Allow to drain for a few minutes, then take up the muslin and squeeze out excess moisture. Gently shape the panir still in the muslin so that it is about 1.5cm (1/2 inch) thick. Place on a hard surface and put a large saucepan filled with water or other heavy object on top to help squeeze out all the moisture. Leave for an hour and cut the panir into cubes.

How to clarify butter to make ghee

Gently heat 500g (1 lb 2 oz) of organic butter in a small saucepan until completely melted. Continue to heat for 15–20 minutes until the solids sink to the bottom. Skim the surface, allow to cool a little, and strain the ghee into a suitable dish.

Other key ingredients

Every region has its favourite ingredients and Indian restaurant cuisine embraces and reflects the flavours and diversity of various regions and cultures throughout India.

Foods of North India

North Indian cuisine possibly influences Indian restaurant cuisine more than any other. A region that enjoys a temperate climate and rich fertile soils, its cuisine is the product of Punjabi and Moghul influences, characterized by the daily consumption of dairy foods: milk, panir, ghee (clarified butter), malai (cream) and yogurt.

North Indian cuisine is recognized by the use of the *tava* (a cast-iron griddle) used for cooking flat breads like roti and paratha, made from locally grown wheat and sometimes corn (maize) and eaten with every meal. Rice is not easily grown in the climate of the region.

Northern India is also home to the *tandoor*. Used for baking breads such as tandoori roti, nan and kulcha and cooking meat dishes like Tandoori Chicken and Seekh Kebab, it has become a trademark of Indian restaurants. Other breads like poori and bhatoora are deep-fried in ghee or oil and are common at festive occasions and street stalls. The population of the region is largely vegetarian but goat and lamb are consumed by a relatively small number of non-vegetarians.

The samosa is a north Indian favourite and now common in other parts of India, Asia and the Middle East, and generally served as an entrée in Indian restaurants. The original samosa was filled with boiled, fried or mashed potato and spices, but other tasty fillings have evolved and now include minced lamb or vegetables. Growing up I can remember making mountains of samosas 'from scratch' for parties and festive occasions – no mean feat by any stretch of the imagination. Now you can buy them freshly cooked in any quantity from Indian sweet shops and cafés. Generally, they are not as good as home-made but I am probably more pedantic than most.

Foods of South India

South Indian cooking boasts the value and versatility of rice as a staple food. The foods of southern India are often more fiery and pungent due to the liberal use of hot red chillies and souring ingredients like tamarind, kokum and lime. Coconut and curry leaves are also used liberally in this region and emerge in various tasteful guises at almost every meal. Cooks in this part of India tend to use spice pastes, moistened with water or oil, while in the north dishes are more often based on dry spice mixes such as garam masala. Some popular dishes include a varied range of biryanis and pilaffs made with locally produced rice.

Foods of West India

Western India has three or four quite distinct food styles, the best known of which is probably Goan, a fusion of local and Portuguese cuisine. The Portuguese, who lived in the area for nearly 500 years, are the major influencers of the cuisine enjoyed up and down the west coast of India. The chilli, which has become synonymous with Indian cuisine, was first introduced to India by the Portuguese. Rice is the staple grain and there is abundant use of fresh coconut and seafood flavoured with fresh herbs and spice mixtures.

Other regions in western India rely more on wheat, corn and maize for staples and use groundnut instead of coconut to add texture and thickness to dishes. To the north of the region, the predominantly vegetarian cuisine of Gujerat has its own distinctive character. Jaggery (boiled-down sugar cane juice) is often used to add sweetness and balance to the pungently spicy staples such as chilli-flecked lentils, and tamarind is used to add a sour tang to vegetable dishes. Turmeric, chillies, cumin and coriander are typically grown in the Gujerat.

Foods of East India

East Indian cuisine is famous for its *mathai* (Indian sweets), particularly milk-based sweets such as the luscious *gulab jamon*, *rasgulla* and *chumchum*. Many of the sweets now popular in northern India originated in this region.

Cashew nut, mustard seed or poppy seed pastes are used for thickening and are definitive of savoury dishes in this part of India, whereas in other regions onions, ginger and garlic mixtures are used to flavour and thicken curry sauces. Fish and seafood are abundant and popular in the coastal states. Smaller fish are made into delicious, spicy soups or deep-fried and eaten with spicy pickles, sauces and chutneys. Larger fish are smothered and marinated with fragrant spice pastes before being lightly steamed or pan-fried.

- **Coriander leaves** – Coriander leaves and coriander seeds are quite dissimilar in taste – although if you pick the seeds while still green they have an intense coriander flavour. The distinct flavour of fresh leaves is incomparable for flavour and aroma. Fresh coriander leaves ground to a paste alone or with mint leaves are a popular base for fresh chutneys. Buy coriander from Indian grocers for a better quality, less expensive product, or grow your own for maximum flavour and freshness.
- **Curry leaves** – Bright green, aromatic leaves that impart a 'curryish' flavour to dishes. Use fresh or dried. Available from ethnic grocers, curry leaves freeze really well.
- **Fenugreek leaves** – Much more robust in flavour and aroma than coriander, fenugreek leaves are a tasty addition to bhajis, pakoras and curries. Fresh fenugreek leaves are readily available from Indian grocers, or can easily be grown from seed. Kasoori methi is sun-dried fenugreek and is a good substitute when fresh fenugreek is not available.
- **Fresh ginger** – Although dried ground ginger is used in a few traditional Indian dishes, it's more usual to cook with fresh ginger root. Look for firm, unwrinkled roots.
- **Chillies** – Chillies come in many shapes, sizes and colours, and vary in heat from quite mild to extremely hot. Generally, the smaller the chilli the hotter it will be. Indian cooks and chefs mostly use fresh green chillies, the red ones being reserved for pickling or drying and pounding to chilli powder. Chillies are easy to grow. Handle cut chillies carefully as the irritant in them causes a burning sensation on contact with the skin. Wash your hands before touching your face.
- **Chat masala** – The most popular and commonly used spice mix for Indian refreshments and snacks, this is a mix of roasted cumin and coriander seeds, chilli, ground black peppercorns, ambchoor, salt and black salt (*sanchal*). Available in small packs from Indian grocers.
- **Ghee** – Ghee is clarified butter. It can be heated to a high temperature without burning and was traditionally prized and used for all cooking, sweet and savoury. Nowadays it is generally

used only at special celebrations such as wedding feasts and religious occasions. Vegetable ghee is often used by Indian restaurant chefs but lacks the flavour of the real thing. At home, sunflower, olive or non-genetically modified canola oil is the preferred cooking medium for everyday meals, and is a healthier option.

- **Gram flour (Besan)** – Chickpea flour is used for bhajis, pakoras, yogurt-based curries and sweetmeats. Best purchased from Indian grocers.
- **Jaggery** – Raw, unrefined sugar with a distinctive taste made from cooked-down sugar cane juice. Muscovado sugar or even dark brown sugar is fine as an alternative.
- **Saffron** – Dried stigmas of crocus flowers, noted for its deep orange colour and sweet delicate aroma. Traditionally used in biryanis and other rice dishes. Needs to be soaked in water or milk before use.
- **Tamarind** – A tart fruit used as a souring agent. Available in pods, blocks or as a concentrate. The concentrate is the most convenient but doesn't have the flavour and texture of the pods and blocks. If you plan to do a lot of cooking using tamarind, buy the block and soak in a little hot water for 20 minutes or so and squeeze out the pulp.
- **Yogurt** – A cooling contrast to spicy dishes, and excellent for cleansing the palate after a hot curry. Home-made yogurt is superior in flavour to shop-bought and is very easy to make. Recipe page 24.
- **Atta** – Chapatti flour is a finely ground, soft wheat flour with varying amounts of wheat bran, from dark wholemeal containing 100 per cent of the bran to the lighter flours with large amounts of the bran removed. Canadian Gold, a new addition to the varieties of atta now available from Indian grocers, is a finely ground flour made from durum wheat and has a pale yellow tinge. The dough made from this flour doesn't need resting, so it is very convenient, but the chapattis don't keep as well. The lighter flours are generally used by restaurant chefs but I prefer the wholemeal for flavour and nutritional value.
- **Basmati rice** – Basmati is the king of rice, with Pakistani basmati rice considered to be the best. It has a nutty flavour and aroma and retains its 'bite' when cooked. Use for savoury and sweet dishes.
- **Food colouring** – Red, yellow and green food colouring is used liberally by Indian chefs. Buy powdered colourings if you wish to use them or substitute with turmeric and paprika. You won't get the deep colour of some of the restaurant dishes, but the flavour will not be affected.
- **Oils** – Mustard seed oil is widely used in India (and has been for centuries) for deep-frying and other cooking uses. The use of good quality, 'healthy' oils, such as olive, safflower and non-GM canola, will ensure that the food you enjoy is also contributing to good health. I use olive oil in most of my savoury recipes as it has a fairly high cooking temperature and adds a nice taste, but this is a matter of personal choice.

Useful utensils

There are a few items of kitchen hardware that make preparing Indian restaurant food easier, less time-consuming and more 'authentic':

■ A deep, heavy-bottomed frying pan or two needs to be top of your list. This enables the curries to be cooked quickly without burning and with even evaporation for thickening the sauces. It can also be used for making chapattis and parathas instead of using a tava (cast-iron griddle).

■ A jug blender is essential if you intend to make the curry sauce on a regular basis. A hand blender will suffice for small quantities although the sauce will not be quite as smooth.

■ A coffee grinder for grinding spices is also a good idea, unless you are a dab hand with a pestle and mortar.

■ A small pestle and mortar is useful for crushing whole spices such as whole cardamoms or coriander seeds.

■ A sizzler dish or two is a must if you like the tandoori dishes served sizzling at the table. You can make do with a cast-iron frying pan if you already have one and if you don't need to impress at the table.

■ A couple of balti dishes will add to the authenticity if you like balti curries.

■ A karahi or wok is useful, particularly if you want to cut down on the amount of oil used. Because of its small base, the cooking oil sits in a small pool at the bottom of the utensil, so you can use a lot less. It is also a good utensil for deep-frying foods such as samosas, pakoras, pooris and bhatooras (breads).

Handy tips, useful shortcuts and tricks of the trade

■ If you don't use up the fresh ginger, chillies and garlic that you have bought, place them all in the jug of your blender or food processor and process until fine. Freeze the mixture in ice-cube trays. Use a cube or two straight from the freezer when required.

■ Fresh green fenugreek left over from a bunch or a good harvest need not be wasted. Wash and dry well, chop and freeze in freezer bags or plastic containers. It doesn't turn into a solid mass, and you can use a little or a lot whenever you want, straight from the freezer.

■ Making samosas and don't want to take the time making and rolling the dough? Use wonton wrappers, spring roll wrappers or even ready-made puff pastry instead. The result will not be 'authentic' but it is a quick and tasty alternative.

■ Buy ready-made panir or try tofu as a substitute. Both are available in blocks from supermarkets and health food shops.

■ Make a double quantity of chapatti or nan dough, let it rest for 10–15 minutes and freeze half. Defrost in the fridge overnight and it will be as good as new.

- Save time by pre-cooking diced vegetables such as carrots and potatoes in boiling salted water or the microwave for a few minutes, until almost tender. Use to make a speedy vegetable bhaji.
- Buy cauliflower when it is in season and cheap, break into florets and wash and drain. Blanch the florets in a large pan of boiling salted water for 2 minutes, drain and immediately immerse in ice cold water to stop the cooking process and maintain a nice colour. Freeze in freezer bags. You can make Aloo Gobi or pakoras in a matter of minutes whenever you want. Restaurant chefs often use frozen cauliflower for speed and convenience.
- Save a little of your tandoori marinade and stir a tablespoonful or so into your curries during the last minute or two of cooking for extra flavour and colour.
- 'Dry' popadoms, after frying in hot oil, upright (in a toast rack or metal colander) in a warm oven for a crisp, non-greasy result.
- Freeze quantities of the curry sauce, chicken and meat, cooked as suggested and you can put your favourite curries together in minutes whenever you feel like an 'Indian'.

GET READY – IN SUMMARY

a) Make a small quantity of garam masala.

b) Prepare ground coriander and cumin.

c) Prepare garlic, ginger and chillies.

d) Have quantities of other essential and key ingredients to hand.

e) Make a quantity of curry sauce (page 32) and freeze it.

a) Garam masala

Garam means 'hot' and *masala* a 'mixture of spices'. According to the Ayurvedic concept of health, food items have differing effects on our bodies and our health due to our constitution or *tri-dosha*. The heat from this 'hot' spice mix is not a heat that you taste as with chillies, but one that warms the body. Spices such as cloves, cinnamon, black cardamoms and nutmeg are the *garam* constituents of this aromatic mixture.

b) Prepare ground Coriander and Cumin

Many recipes call for the use of coriander and cumin powder. Having the spices ground and ready to use makes life a lot easier.

GARAM MASALA

Makes about 3 tablespoonfuls

1 tbsp coriander seeds
1 tbsp cumin
1 tsp green cardamoms
1 tsp cloves
1 tsp black peppercorns
2 sticks of cinnamon, about 5cm (2 inches) in length
2 bay leaves
1/2 small nutmeg
4 black cardamoms

Place all the ingredients into an electric coffee-grinder and grind to a fine powder. Carefully remove the lid and test by rubbing a little of the mixture between forefinger and thumb. Finely ground spices should not feel gritty. If necessary, grind for another few seconds. Alternatively, grind to a fine powder in a pestle and mortar.

Store the ground spices in a small non-corrosive, airtight container and remember to label it.

Place 2 or 3 tablespoonfuls of coriander seeds into the bowl of a coffee grinder and grind to a fine powder. Store in a small airtight container and label. Repeat with 2 or 3 tablespoonfuls of cumin seeds.

c) Prepare Garlic, Ginger and Chillies
Many of the dishes in this book require the use of finely chopped garlic, ginger and green chillies. If you plan to do much Indian cooking, it is helpful to have a quantity of these ready prepared so that you can put a meal together with the maximum of ease.

d) Have quantities of the other essential and key ingredients to hand
Ingredients such as turmeric, chilli powder, paprika, cardamom pods, cinnamon and cloves are common items in Indian restaurant cooking. Have small amounts available at all times to make preparing your favourite dishes easy.

e) Make a quantity of Curry Sauce and freeze it
The basis for many of the curries in this book, the curry sauce makes preparing curries simplicity itself. See page 32 for the new, no smell curry sauce that is even better than the original *Curry Secret* curry sauce.

GARLIC, GINGER AND CHILLIES

Separate the cloves from 2 bulbs of garlic and peel.

Peel 300g (11 oz) fresh ginger and roughly chop.

Place the garlic cloves and ginger in a food processor or blender and process until finely chopped.

Take an ice-cube tray and put 2 teaspoonfuls of the mixture into each section.

Freeze until solid.

Remove the cubes of mix and place in a freezer bag or plastic container and store in the freezer.

One 'cube' or 'portion' is approximately equivalent to 2 cloves of garlic and a 2.5cm (1 inch) piece of ginger, the quantity and proportions used in most recipes, and can be used straight from the freezer or thawed in the microwave.

Green chillies – Repeat the above process with a quantity of green chillies. You probably require only half a cube of chillies for most recipes, but how much you use will depend on how hot the chillies are. Start with less, and add more if you want more heat.

6. WEIGHTS AND MEASURES

Both metric and imperial measurements have been given in this book with the imperial measures being rounded up or down to the nearest unit. Remember to use one or the other and not to combine imperial and metric measurements in one recipe.

All spoon measurements throughout the book are **slightly rounded** spoonfuls (American readers please note) unless specified as being level.

Fluid ounces refer to the British fluid ounce, which is slightly smaller than the US equivalent. This difference is not significant for the recipes in this book.

Cup size is the metric cup (250ml) or half a US pint.

Some conversions are given in the tables below:

Measure	UK	USA	Australia
Teaspoon	5ml	4.9ml	5ml
Dessertspoon	10ml	—	10ml
Tablespoon	15ml	14.8ml	20ml
Cup	285ml	236.6ml	250ml (metric cup)
Fluid oz	28.4ml	29.6ml	—
1 litre	2.2 pints	2.1 pints	—

KILOGRAMS, POUNDS AND OUNCES

1 ounce (abbreviated oz) = approximately 28g
1 lb (16 oz) = approximately 453g
1 kilo = 2 lb 4 oz
500g = 1 lb 2 oz

7.

THE NEW CURRY SAUCE,
SMELLS GOOD DURING COOKING

THIS IS the foundation of many of the curries served in Indian restaurants and is prepared in abundance and regularity by Indian chefs. Its recipe and method of preparation is also the most closely guarded secret of restaurant cooking. Indian cooking does not employ thickeners such as flour or cornflour, instead relying upon onions, ginger and garlic to give the sauce its substance, flavour and texture.

If you have purchased preparations of curry sauces from supermarkets or grocers and been grossly disappointed with the end result, this recipe will be manna from heaven. This is the real thing. Have some of this curry sauce on hand, and you can prepare a delicious Indian meal within minutes, just like the experts.

The curry sauce is simple to make, and this method of making it, although different from the way it is made in many restaurants, smells pleasant during cooking. It keeps for up to four days in the fridge and can be frozen in serving-size portions for ultimate convenience.

These quantities make enough curry sauce for about eight main course dishes.

Preparation and cooking time: about 1½ hours	4 tbsp olive oil	1.5 litres (53 fl oz/3 US pints) water
	1 kg (2 lb 4 oz) onions, sliced	1 can (225g/8 oz) tomatoes
	1 tsp salt	1 tsp tomato paste (tomato purée double concentrate)
	50g (about 2 oz) fresh ginger, coarsely chopped	1 tsp turmeric
	50g (2 oz) garlic, coarsely chopped	1 tsp paprika

Step 1

■ Heat all but 1 tablespoonful of the oil in a large saucepan with a tight-fitting lid, and add the sliced onions. Stir on high heat for a minute or two and then turn the heat down a little. Continue to cook the onion, stirring frequently, for about 10 minutes until the onion is transparent and beginning to brown at the edges.

■ Add the salt, stir well and turn the heat down to as low as you can. Cover pan and continue to cook the onion for about 20 minutes, stirring three or four times during that period. The addition of salt will prevent the onion from browning and help it soften and break down, but be careful it does not stick to the bottom of the pan.

■ Add the ginger and garlic to the onion. Turn the heat up a little and cook for a minute or two, until aromatic.

■ Add the water and bring to the boil. Turn the heat down and simmer the mixture, partly covered, for 20–25 minutes.

■ Leave to cool.

Step 2

■ Once cooled, ladle half the mixture into a blender jug and blend until smooth. To ensure that the sauce is really smooth, blend for about 2 minutes. Pour the blended onion mixture into a clean pan or bowl and repeat with the other half of the onion mixture.

■ Wash and dry the saucepan. Reserve about 4 tablespoonfuls of the sauce at this point to use for cooking the meat as detailed in many of the recipes in this book.

Freezing: Freeze at this stage if you want to keep the sauce for up to 2 months. You can freeze the finished sauce for up to 1 month.

Step 3

■ Place the contents of the can of tomatoes into the rinsed blender jug and blend until smooth, for about 2 minutes.

■ Place the cleaned saucepan onto medium heat and heat the remaining oil. Add the tomato paste, turmeric and paprika and cook for about 30 seconds. Add the blended tomatoes and bring to the boil. Turn down the heat and cook, stirring occasionally, for about 10 minutes.

■ Add the blended onion mixture to the tomatoes and bring to the boil again. Turn down the heat so that the sauce simmers gently.

■ As the sauce simmers, you will notice froth rises to the surface. This needs to be skimmed off. Continue to simmer, skimming as necessary, for 20–25 minutes.

■ Use immediately or cool and refrigerate for up to 4 days. Freeze for up to 1 month.

TIP

If you wish to speed things up a little, you can eliminate Step 3. Simply add the spices, tomato paste and canned tomatoes to the onions in Step 1, just before adding the water. Simmer for about 10 minutes before adding the water and proceed as suggested. Beware, though, that your blender jug will take on the yellow colour of the turmeric. This will wash off more easily if you use a little dishwasher powder or laundry detergent dissolved in hot water.

8. ENTRÉES AND LIGHT LUNCHES

THE RICHNESS and diversity of Indian food are no more adequately reflected than in the enormous array of snacks, appetizers, hors d'oeuvres and tasty little titbits enjoyed by millions of Indians every day. Each region of India has its own local specialities but they are all tantalizingly spicy, delicious, inexpensive and readily available.

A variety of particularly common and popular snacks eaten throughout India are referred to as *chats*. Chana Chat Masala, Chicken Chat and Aloo Chat are all chats served in Indian restaurants, but there are many more varieties. A hot, tangy and sweet mix of tastes that once acquired is forever desired.

The majority of traditional snacks are potato based. The Aloo Ki Tikki for example, one of the oldest Indian snacks recorded in history, is made from mashed, spiced potatoes.

THE SAMOSA
Another popular snack, and one reportedly enjoyed by the British during the Raj, is the ubiquitous spicy little pastry triangle know as the samosa. It is believed that the samosa originated in Central Asia before the tenth century and made its way to India via ancient trade routes such as the Old Silk Road. The samosa is now a popular snack all over the world.

Traditionally, samosas were made with potatoes, spices and vegetables. Modern-day Indian cuisine incorporates meat, fish and cheese into some of the original samosa recipes.

MAKING SAMOSAS 'FROM SCRATCH'
A common practice not all that long ago, it is now a rarity to make samosas at home. And it's no wonder: it's a time- and effort-consuming task, particularly when making large amounts. Recipes and methods of preparation vary slightly from one household to another but all require the following steps:

- Preparing and cooking the potato or meat filling
- Preparing the pastry dough
- Rolling the pastry
- Filling the pastry
- Deep-frying

Freshly made samosas are available readily and cheaply from Indian snack and sweet shops, and the vast majority of people, including many restaurant chefs, take the route of least inconvenience and buy them ready-made. However, the quality can be inconsistent. Home-made samosas are generally the best.

SERVING INDIAN SNACKS AND STARTERS

Traditionally, there is no proper or right way to serve Indian food; although in Indian restaurants in the West it is common to eat two or more 'courses'. The dishes on the next pages can be served as starters if you wish to introduce a little formality into your occasion, or may form part of the main meal with a selection of dishes on the table at the same time. They also make delicious snacks at any time of the day. The important thing is to cook good food and enjoy it with family and friends.

Non-vegetarian starters menu

Lamb Boti
Chunks of tender lamb marinated in a mix of fresh ginger, garlic, chilli and lemon juice.

Meat Samosa with Kashmiri Chat
Spicy minced lamb enclosed in a crisp light pastry served with chickpeas in a tamarind sauce.

Spicy Lamb Cutlets
Garlicky, spicy lamb cutlets, marinated in fresh herbs and grilled until sizzling.

Kashmiri Lamb Cutlets
Meltingly tender lamb cutlets enclosed in a crisp, spicy golden coating.

Murgh Seekh Kebab
Minced chicken combined with fresh coriander, spring onions, herbs and spices.

Murgh Tikka Hariyali
Tender breast pieces marinated in mint, green chillies and spices.

Chicken Dosai
Thin golden rice pancakes enclosing a filling of mustard-flavoured shredded chicken.

Fish Pakora
Pieces of fresh fish, dipped in a gram flour batter flavoured with spices and herbs.

Ajwaini King Prawns
King prawns tossed with carom seeds, coriander and cumin served with char-grilled orange slices.

LAMB BOTI

Traditionally, this dish uses cubed leg of lamb, marinated in spices and yogurt that tenderize and flavour the meat. It is then skewered and cooked over hot coals (or in the tandoor), creating lovely crispy bits on the outside of the meat while the inside is deliciously moist and tender. You can achieve similar results on a barbecue, failing which a really hot oven or griller will be fine.

SERVES 4

Preparation and cooking time: 25–30 minutes (meat requires marinating overnight)

350g (12 oz) lean lamb taken from the leg
2 cloves of garlic, minced or finely chopped
Small piece of ginger, grated
  (or a portion of prepared garlic and ginger mix,
  page 30, thawed)
1 tbsp chopped coriander
$1/2$ tsp turmeric
$1/2$ tsp ground coriander

$1/2$ tsp ground cumin
$1/2$ tsp garam masala
1 tsp chilli powder
Juice of half a lemon or lime
2 tbsp yogurt
1 tbsp oil
1 tsp salt

■ Cut the lamb into 2.5cm (1 inch) chunks, place in a deep bowl and sprinkle on all the remaining ingredients except the yogurt, oil and salt.

■ Stir and turn the meat pieces until evenly coated with herbs and spices. Add the yogurt and oil and mix well. Cover and marinate the meat overnight in the fridge.

■ Pre-heat the oven (at 230°C, 450° F or gas mark 8), barbecue or grill. Remove the meat from the fridge about 30 minutes before cooking.

■ Sprinkle the salt onto the meat and mix well. Thread the meat onto metal skewers (or pre-soaked wooden skewers), keeping the meat pieces about 1cm ($1/2$ inch) apart. Reserve the marinade.

■ Cook the lamb in the oven for about 20–25 minutes, or on the barbecue or under the grill for about 15 minutes, turning once and brushing with the marinade half way through cooking.

■ Serve with a crisp green salad and yogurt mint sauce (page 40).

MEAT SAMOSA WITH KASHMIRI CHAT

This can be served as a hearty starter, a tasty snack with drinks or a light lunch. The fresh-tasting Kashmiri Chat incorporates sweet, hot and sour flavours and goes particularly well with these spicy samosas.

MAKES 12 SAMOSAS

Preparation and cooking time: 45 minutes (with ready prepared filling)

150g (5 oz) plain flour
1/2 tsp salt
1 tbsp olive oil
120ml (about 4 fl oz) water
1 quantity of Karahi Keema (page 96)
Oil for deep-frying

■ To make the pastry dough, sift the flour and salt into a bowl. Make a well in the centre of the flour and add the oil.

■ Add the water, a little at a time starting at the centre to incorporate the oil and mix, bringing the flour together until you have a soft, pliable dough.

■ Knead gently for a minute or two. Cover and leave to rest for about 10 minutes.

■ Divide the mixture into 6 portions. Take one portion, roll between floured hands to make a ball. Flatten slightly and roll into a circle about 20cm (8 inches) in diameter.

■ Cut each circle in half, and then taking the two corners of one half, bring the cut sides together, slightly overlapping, to make a hollow cone. Seal by pressing the cut sides together. You may need to dampen the edges with a little water.

■ Fill about three-quarters full with the Keema mixture, being careful not to overfill. Pinch the open ends together firmly to enclose. Set aside and repeat with remaining dough.

■ Deep-fry in batches and drain on a wire rack. Keep warm in a low oven while cooking the remaining samosas.

Kashmiri Chat

1 heaped tsp tamarind paste
100ml (about 3 fl oz) water
1 can (425g/15 oz) chick peas, drained
1 small red onion, finely diced
1 tomato, de-seeded and the flesh diced
1 green chilli, finely chopped
1 tsp Kashmiri chilli powder, or $1/2$ tsp red chilli powder
$1/2$ tsp garam masala
1 tsp chat masala
1 tsp salt
1 tbsp tomato ketchup
1 tbsp chopped coriander

Dissolve the tamarind in the water and place all the other ingredients in a bowl. Mix well.

If using a block of tamarind for the Kashmiri Chat, soak a golf-ball size piece in 120ml (4 fl oz) of hot water for 20–30 minutes. Squeeze out the pulp and discard solids and seeds.

Note: Kashmiri chilli powder is redder but milder than ordinary chilli powder.

TIP

Make the chat the day before and allow the flavours to develop.

SPICY LAMB CUTLETS

These lamb cutlets are so succulent and tasty you will have everyone coming back for more.
The cutlets come from the rib and contain the tender fillet attached to the rib bone which
makes them ideal as a finger food for informal gatherings.

SERVES 4

Preparation and cooking time: approximately 30 minutes (plus 2–3 hours marinating time)

8 lamb cutlets
2 tbsp finely chopped mint leaves (or 2 heaped tsp mint jelly out of a jar)
1 tsp chilli powder
1 tsp paprika
3 cloves of garlic, minced or finely chopped
1 tsp ground cumin

1 tsp ground coriander
Juice of half a lemon
1 tbsp olive oil
1 tbsp mint jelly
1 tsp salt

- Trim the cutlets and scrape the bone ends to remove fat and gristle.

- Mix all the remaining ingredients except the salt in a bowl, and add the lamb cutlets. Using your hands rub the herb and spice mixture into the meat ensuring each cutlet is evenly coated. Cover and leave to marinate in the fridge for at least 2 hours or overnight.

- Remove the lamb from the fridge about half an hour before cooking.

- Heat a heavy-based frying pan, capable of holding the cutlets without overcrowding, until very hot.

- Sprinkle some salt onto each cutlet. Cook the cutlets for about 1½ minutes each side.

- Serve hot with yogurt mint sauce.

YOGURT MINT SAUCE

150ml (5 fl oz) plain yogurt
1 tsp mint sauce
½ level tsp salt
¼ tsp chilli powder
¼ tsp garam masala
¼ tsp ambchoor
½ tsp caster sugar
2 tsp chopped fresh mint (optional)

Place all the ingredients in a bowl and mix well.

TIPS

The mint jelly is the secret ingredient in this dish. The hint of
sweetness balances the lemon juice and spices beautifully.

Ready prepared garlic, usually preserved in lemon juice, is
also a good shortcut for marinades requiring lots of garlic.

KASHMIRI LAMB CUTLETS

This is an unusual but absolutely delicious dish of pre-cooked, tender lamb cutlets, enclosed in a golden, crispy batter.

SERVES 4

Preparation and cooking time: 45–50 minutes

8 lamb cutlets
200ml (7 fl oz) milk
1/2 tsp garam masala
3 cloves
6 cardamom pods
1 tsp grated ginger
1 tbsp chopped onion
sprinkling of salt

3 tbsp gram flour (besan)
1 tbsp rice flour
1 tsp chilli powder
1/2 tsp paprika
1/2 tsp salt
1/2 tsp turmeric
1/4 tsp ground methi (fenugreek) leaves (optional)
Oil for deep-frying

Step 1

■ Trim the cutlets and scrape the bone end of each cutlet. Place the milk, garam masala, cloves, cardamoms, ginger and onion in a pan large enough to hold the cutlets in a single layer, and bring to the boil.

■ Add the cutlets, bring the milk back to the boil, turn down the heat and simmer gently for about 20 minutes, turning once or twice, until the cutlets are tender and all the liquid has evaporated.

■ Sprinkle the cutlets with a little salt each side, remove from the pan and cool.

■ Cutlets can be prepared to this stage up to 24 hours ahead.

Step 2

■ Combine the gram flour, rice flour, chilli powder, paprika, salt, turmeric and methi, if using, in a bowl. Add enough water to make a thickish batter. Allow to stand for at least 10 minutes.

■ Dip the lamb cutlets in the batter, shaking off the excess and fry in hot oil until crisp and golden.

■ Drain on kitchen paper and serve with spicy peach chutney (page 172) or yogurt mint sauce (page 40).

TIP

The rice flour helps makes the batter crisper but it is not essential. Use extra besan flour if you don't have it.

MURGH SEEKH KEBAB

Made with lean minced chicken and fresh herbs, these tasty kebabs make a nice change from the traditional lamb 'Seekh Kebabs'.

SERVES 4	2 spring onions, finely sliced	225g (8 oz) minced chicken
Preparation and cooking time: 20–25 minutes	2 tbsp chopped coriander	1 tsp salt
	2 green chillies, finely chopped	1 tsp garam masala
	2 tsp fresh ginger, grated	Juice of half a lemon
	3 cloves of garlic, finely chopped	1 egg, lightly beaten

BE A SIZZLER

- Heat a sizzler dish on a gas flame for about 5 minutes until very hot.
- Turn down the heat and place some sliced onion onto the dish.
- Immediately place the cooked food on top of the onion.
- Drizzle a little oil onto the side of the dish and tilt it slightly so the oil runs across the dish. It will start sizzling.
- Now drizzle some lemon juice onto the onions. This produces even more sizzling and a delicious aroma.
- Finally, sprinkle with chopped coriander, and serve.

■ Preheat the oven to its maximum temperature, or turn on the grill to heat. Place all the ingredients into a large bowl, and using your hands mix thoroughly.

■ Divide the mixture into 8 equal parts, and using oiled hands form into sausage shapes about 10cm (4 inches) in length.

■ Place these on a rack in a shallow baking tray and cook near the top of the oven for 10–12 minutes, or under a very hot grill for 8–10 minutes, turning once.

■ Serve sizzling with a green salad, yogurt mint sauce (page 40) and a wedge of lemon.

TIP

Place the first five ingredients, roughly chopped, into the bowl of a small food processor and process for a few seconds until finely chopped. Combine with the remaining ingredients and proceed as above.

MURGH TIKKA HARIYALI

Chicken tikka with fresh green (*hariyali*) herbs appears to be a Bengali dish, although the Punjabis also claim it as their own. Beautifully spiced, aromatic with fresh herbs, it will stimulate your tastebuds and your appetite. It's easy to prepare and very tasty.

SERVES 4–6

Preparation and cooking time: 30 minutes (plus marinating time of 2–3 hours or overnight)

3 chicken fillets
Juice of half a lemon or lime
1 tsp salt
3 tbsp coriander leaves
3 tbsp mint leaves
4 or 5 fresh curry leaves
3 or 4 green garlic tops (optional)

2 green chillies
2.5cm (1 inch) ginger, roughly chopped
2 cloves of garlic, roughly chopped
1 tsp garam masala
2 tbsp yogurt
1 tbsp oil plus extra for basting

- Rinse the chicken fillets, pat dry with paper towels, and cut into 4cm (1½ inch) chunks. Sprinkle on the lemon or lime juice and salt, stir well and set aside.

- Place the herbs, chillies, ginger, garlic, garam masala, yogurt and oil into the bowl of a blender or food processor and process to a coarse paste.

- Add the herb paste to the chicken, mix well and refrigerate for 2–3 hours or overnight to marinate.

- Remove the chicken from the fridge at least half an hour before cooking and insert onto metal or pre-soaked wooden skewers.

- Heat the grill or barbecue and cook the chicken skewers for 12–15 minutes, basting once or twice with a little oil and turning frequently until cooked through.

- Serve hot with mango chutney (page 171) and lemon wedges.

TIP

You can brown the chicken pieces in a very hot frying pan, then, using kitchen tongs, skewer them and bake in a hot oven (220°C, 425°F or gas mark 7) for 15 minutes.

CHICKEN DOSAI

The dosai, or dosa as it is commonly known in the West, originates from south India although it is popular all over the country. Dosai are made from a batter of soaked, ground and fermented rice and urad dhal, which is poured onto a tava (cast-iron griddle) and fried in oil or ghee, rather like a pancake or crepe. Traditionally dosai are served with a variety of chutneys and eaten for breakfast. In the West it is more usual to eat dosai stuffed with spicy potato or meat fillings, more commonly referred to as 'Masala Dosai'.

Making the dosai batter at home is a lengthy and laborious process. The quick and convenient way is to buy the ready prepared mix, which is very good and available from Indian grocers. Simply add the filling of your choice. Making dosai takes a little practice, so be prepared to throw the first couple away. Starting with a warm rather than hot pan makes it easier and practice makes perfect.

SERVES 4	2 tbsp olive oil	2–3 green chillies, finely sliced
	1 tsp black mustard seeds	1 tsp salt
Preparation and cooking time: approximately 45 minutes	2 onions, sliced	1/2 tsp turmeric
	4 or 5 curry leaves, fresh or dried	225g (8 oz) chicken, thinly sliced
	2 cloves of garlic, finely chopped	1 tsp garam masala
	2.5cm (1 inch) ginger, finely chopped	1 tbsp coriander leaves
	(or a portion of prepared garlic and ginger mix, page 30, thawed)	1 pkt of dosai mix
		About 2 tbsp oil extra

■ Heat the oil in a medium saucepan. When hot throw in the mustard seeds, shake the pan for 2 or 3 seconds until they pop and quickly add the onions followed by the curry leaves.

■ Cook on medium to high heat until the onions are translucent and add the garlic, ginger and chillies. Stir-fry for a minute or two.

■ Add the salt and turmeric, stir and add in the chicken. Continue stirring on medium to high heat until the chicken begins to colour.

■ Add 4 tablespoonfuls of water, cover the pan, turn down the heat and cook for 10 minutes, stirring occasionally.

Sambhar

$1/2$ tsp fenugreek seeds
$1/2$ tsp coriander seeds
$1/2$ tsp cumin seeds
$1/2$ tsp black peppercorns
6 dried red chillies
3 tsp tamarind paste
200ml (7 fl oz) warm water
200g (7 oz) red lentils
200g (7 oz) chopped mixed vegetables
$1/2$ tsp turmeric
500ml (18 fl oz) cold water
1 tbsp oil
$1/2$ tsp black mustard seeds
8 curry leaves
1 medium onion, chopped
pinch asafoetida (optional)
1 ripe tomato, chopped
2 tsp salt (or to taste)
2 tbsp chopped coriander

In a small pan dry-roast the fenugreek, coriander, cumin, peppercorns and chillies until aromatic. Remove from the pan, cool and grind to a powder.

Dissolve the tamarind in about 200ml (7 fl oz) of warm water. Set aside.

Meanwhile, wash and drain the lentils and combine with the vegetables, turmeric and 500ml (18 fl oz) of water. Bring to the boil, skim the froth off the top and simmer for 30 minutes, stirring now and again.

In a separate pan, heat the oil and add the mustard seeds and curry leaves. Cook for a minute and stir in the onion and asafoetida if using.

Stir-fry the onion until starting to colour and add the tamarind water. Bring to the boil and simmer for 5 minutes.

Add the onion mixture to the dhal (pulses) and vegetables with the tomato, salt and roasted spice mix. Bring back to the boil and simmer for a further 5 minutes.

Stir in the coriander and serve with dosai.

■   Remove the lid and cook on low heat for a further 5 minutes until the mixture is dry and the chicken cooked.

■   Stir in the garam masala and coriander leaves.

■   For dosai, follow instructions on the packet to make the batter and allow to stand for 5 minutes. Set the oven to warm.

■   Warm a frying pan that is about 20–25cm (8–10 inches) in diameter and generously brush or spray with oil.

■   Pour a little batter into the pan and, using a circular motion, spread it around with the back of a spoon.

■   Cook on medium heat and, while the dosai cooks, sprinkle or spray some more oil onto the top and around the edges so that it seeps under the dosai. It will take around 4 minutes to cook.

■   When the edges start to brown, carefully lift the dosai onto an ovenproof platter. Place some filling along the centre of the dosa, and fold over one side and then the other. Hold down for a few seconds to set the dosai in shape.

■   Place in the oven to keep warm while making more dosai.

■   Serve warm with coconut and mint chutney (page 173) and sambhar.

> **TIP**
>
> Have two pans going at the same time, so that you have a cooler one for starting each dosai. Take your time spreading the batter and don't worry if your dosai has large holes or spaces in it. The edges of these holes will get nice and crisp and make it taste even better.

FISH PAKORA

Succulent, creamy chunks of fish enclosed in spicy, crisp, golden batter; equally at home as a snack with tomato ketchup or as an elegant starter, with baby salad leaves, sweet chilli sauce and a wedge of lime.

SERVES 4		
Preparation and cooking time: 25–30 minutes	120g (4 oz) gram flour (besan) 30g (1 oz) rice flour 1 tsp salt 1 green chilli, finely chopped 1/2 tsp chilli powder 1 heaped tsp mint sauce	1/2 tsp garam masala 1/2 tsp ground methi (fenugreek) leaves (optional) 225–280g (8–10 oz) piece of firm white fish 1 tbsp finely chopped coriander Oil for deep-frying

- Sieve the gram flour, rice flour and salt into a large bowl. Add enough water to make into a thick batter.

- Stir in the salt, chilli and chilli powder, mint sauce, garam masala and methi, if using. Allow the batter to stand while preparing the fish.

- Rinse the fish, pat dry with kitchen paper, and cut into large chunks about 5cm (2 inches) in size.

- Stir the coriander into the batter, followed by the fish pieces. Stir the fish around in the batter until each piece is well coated.

- Shake off excess batter, and deep-fry the fish pieces in hot oil for 3–4 minutes until the coating is a rich golden brown and the fish is cooked through.

- Serve hot.

TIPS

- Use any leftover batter for Vegetable Pakora. Simply dip bite-sized pieces of cauliflower, potato, mushroom or aubergine into the batter and deep-fry until crisp. Or stir in some sliced onion or spinach, and drop spoonfuls into hot oil.
- If you have some fresh fenugreek, stir into the batter with the spices; it is wonderful in this dish.

Ajwaini King Prawns

King prawns are fished from various warm waters around the world and are available pre-cooked, and 'green' (raw) if you are fortunate enough to live close to fish markets. If buying frozen prawns, allow plenty of time for defrosting. The best way of defrosting them is slowly in the fridge.

This is an impressive dish that is bursting with flavour. It is delicately yet distinctly spiced with the unique flavour of carom seeds and the tangy sweetness of the orange.

SERVES 4		
Preparation and cooking time: 30 minutes including marinating time	16 king prawns 1 tsp carom seeds (ajwain) 1 tsp ground cumin 1 tsp ground coriander 1/2 tsp turmeric 1 green chilli, finely chopped	1 tbsp finely chopped coriander 1 tsp olive oil Zest of half an orange 1 tsp salt 1 orange, sliced

- If using fresh prawns, shell and de-vein them, leaving the tail intact. Rinse under cold water, drain and pat dry with paper towels.

- Mix all the remaining ingredients, except for the salt and the sliced orange, in a non-corrosive bowl and add the prawns. Stir to coat and leave to marinate for 15 minutes.

- Heat a heavy-based frying pan large enough to take the prawns in a single layer.
Stir the salt into the prawns, cook them over medium heat for about 5 minutes, turning once or twice.

- Meanwhile, char-grill the orange slices on a griddle pan, a minute each side.

- Serve the prawns, sizzling if liked (see page 42), with a green salad, the char-grilled orange slices and coriander and mint drizzle.

Coriander and Mint Drizzle

Take a handful of fresh coriander and mint, one or two green chillies, juice of a lemon, 1 teaspoonful of caster sugar and salt and pepper to taste, and place in a blender.

Blend until smooth.

Vegetarian starters menu

Spinach Bhaji
Shredded spinach, combined with gram flour, herbs and spices, deep-fried until golden.

Vegetarian Samosa
Spicy, tangy potatoes enclosed in a light, crisp pastry.

Vegetarian Dosai
Thin, golden rice pancakes filled with spiced mustard potatoes, served with a *nariyal* (coconut) and mint chutney.

Panir Shashlik
Cubes of home-made cheese, marinated with a blend of herbs and spices, cooked with onions and sweet peppers.

Spring Rolls
Spring roll wrappers filled with finely diced vegetables and panir, lightly spiced and deep-fried until golden.

Aloo Ki Tikki
Crisp, golden potato patties, lightly spiced and flavoured with fresh herbs. Served with a tamarind sauce.

Dhal Soup
A combination of vegetables and lentils in a mildly spiced soup.

SPINACH BHAJI

Spinach Bhaji, or 'Palak Pakorah' as it is referred to in India, is just one of the many types of spicy snacks made with gram (besan) flour. It is quick, easy and tasty and in fact quite nutritious. A good starter or snack for vegetarians and non-vegetarians alike.

SERVES 4–6	225g (8 oz) gram flour (besan)	2 tbsp tomato purée (optional)
Preparation and cooking time: 20–25 minutes	2 tsp salt 1 tsp garam masala 1 or 2 green chillies, finely chopped (or half a portion of prepared chillies, page 30)	1 bunch (about 200g/7 oz) spinach leaves Oil for deep-frying

■ Place all the ingredients except the spinach in a bowl and add enough water to make a thick batter. Cover and leave to stand while preparing the spinach.

■ Wash the spinach leaves in plenty of water, squeeze out excess water and shred the leaves finely. Add to the batter and stir well.

■ Deep-fry tablespoonfuls of the mixture in hot oil. Do not overcrowd the pan. Press the bhaji lightly while it is frying to squeeze the uncooked mixture to the outside and ensure thorough cooking.

■ Drain on paper towels and serve hot with sauce or chutney of choice.

TIP

Use frozen, thawed spinach for added convenience.

VEGETARIAN SAMOSA

The ubiquitous samosa is a popular snack throughout India and famous around the world. A delightful crisp, deep-fried triangle with a delicious spicy filling, it is versatile enough for a quick snack on the run or as part of a prestigious banquet.

The carrots used in this recipe give the filling added flavour and texture, but you can omit them and make up the quantity with more potato.

MAKES 12 SAMOSAS

Preparation and cooking time:
• filling 25–30 minutes
• pastry and remaining process 40–45 minutes

Filling
50g (2 oz) diced carrot
150g (5 oz) diced potato
2 tbsp olive oil
1 onion, finely sliced
2cm (1 inch) piece of ginger, grated or finely chopped
1 or 2 green chillies, finely chopped
1/2 tsp turmeric
1/2 tsp cumin seeds
1 tsp salt

3 tbsp frozen peas
1 tsp ambchoor or juice of half a lemon
1/2 tsp garam masala

Pastry
150g (5 oz) plain flour
1/2 tsp salt
1 tbsp olive oil
120ml (4 fl oz) water
Oil for deep-frying

TAMARIND SAUCE

2 tsp tamarind paste
200ml (7 fl oz) warm water
1/2 tsp salt
1/2 tsp chilli powder
1/2 tsp garam masala
1/2 tsp ambchoor
1 tbsp tomato ketchup
1 carrot, grated
1 tbsp diced red onion
1 tbsp chopped coriander

Dissolve the tamarind paste in the water.

Add the remaining ingredients and mix to combine.

■ Make the filling first. Boil the carrot in salted water for 5 minutes and add the potato. Cook until the vegetables are tender but not breaking apart. Drain.

■ Meanwhile, heat the oil in a heavy-based saucepan and add the onion. Fry for a few minutes over medium heat until the onion is beginning to colour around the edges.

■ Add the ginger, chillies, turmeric, cumin and salt and stir-fry for 2 minutes. Stir in the cooked vegetables, peas, ambchoor and garam masala. Mix well over low heat for a few minutes so that the vegetables absorb the spices.

■ Turn off the heat and allow the filling to cool while making the pastry.

■ To make the pastry dough, sift the flour and salt into a bowl. Make a well in the centre of the flour and add the oil. Add about 120ml (about 4 fl oz) of water, a little at a time starting at the centre to incorporate the oil, and mix, bringing the flour together until you have a soft, pliable dough. Knead gently for a minute or two until smooth.

■ Cover and leave to rest for about 10 minutes.

■ With floured hands, divide the mixture into 6 portions. Take one portion and roll between floured hands to make a ball. Flatten slightly and roll into a thin circle about 20cm (8 inches) in diameter.

■ Cut each circle in half and, taking the two corners of one half, bring the cut sides together, slightly overlapping, to make a hollow cone. Seal by pressing the cut sides together. You may need to dampen the edges with a little water.

■ Fill about three-quarters full with the potato mixture, being careful not to overfill. Pinch the open ends together firmly to enclose the filling. Set aside and repeat with the remaining dough.

■ Deep-fry in batches and drain on a wire rack. Keep warm in a low oven while cooking the remaining samosas.

■ Serve piping hot with Tamarind Sauce, Kashmiri Chat (page 39) or tomato ketchup.

VEGETARIAN DOSAI

This is a delicious and quite substantial dish with a lovely combination of textures and flavours: crispy pancake, moist filling, a fresh tasting chutney and an earthy, tangy sambhar (page 45). For some tips on making the dosai, see Chicken Dosai recipe (page 44).

SERVES 4 **Preparation and cooking time: 45 minutes**	2 tbsp olive oil 1 tsp black mustard seeds 1 onion, sliced 4–5 curry leaves, fresh, frozen or dried 2 green chillies, finely chopped 1/2 tsp ground cumin	1/2 tsp ground coriander 1/2 tsp turmeric 1 1/2 tsp salt 300g (11 oz) diced potato 1 pkt dosai mix

■ Heat the oil in a heavy-based pan and add the mustard seeds. Shake the pan over the heat for a couple of seconds until the seeds pop and immediately add the onion and curry leaves.

■ Cook, stirring over medium to high heat until the onion is translucent, after about 5 minutes. Add the chillies, cumin, coriander, turmeric and salt. Stir for a few seconds until aromatic and add the potato.

■ Stir-fry the potato in the oil and spice mix for 3–4 minutes and add 3 tablespoonfuls of water. Stir again, cover and allow to cook over low heat for about 10–15 minutes until the potato pieces are tender.

■ For the dosai, follow instructions on the packet to make the batter and allow to stand for 5 minutes. Set the oven onto warm.

■ Gently warm a frying pan about 20–25cm (8–10 inches) in diameter and generously brush or spray with oil. Pour a little batter into the pan and, using a circular motion, spread it around with the back of a spoon.

■ Cook on medium heat for about 4 minutes. While the dosai cooks, sprinkle or spray some oil onto the top and around the edges so that it seeps under the dosai.

■ When the edges start to brown, carefully lift the dosai onto an ovenproof platter. Place some filling along the centre of the dosai, and fold over one side and then the other. Hold down for a few seconds and it will hold its shape.

■ Keep warm while making more dosai. Serve warm with coconut and mint chutney (page 173) and sambhar (page 45).

TIP

Have two pans going at the same time, so that you have a cool one for starting each dosai.

PANIR SHASHLIK

Panir or curd is used for a variety of Indian dishes both sweet and savoury, particularly in northern India. It is rich in protein, making it a good substitute for meat in vegetarian meals. This dish is a tasty and colourful starter.

SERVES 4		
Preparation and cooking time: 20–25 minutes (marinating time 2–3 hours)	225g (8 oz) panir (page 24) 1 green capsicum 1 red capsicum 1 onion 2 firm tomatoes 150ml (5 fl oz) plain yogurt 1/2 tsp salt 1 tsp turmeric	2 green chillies, finely chopped (or half a portion of prepared chillies, page 30) 1/2 tsp ground cumin 1/2 tsp ground black pepper 1 tbsp chopped coriander 1 tbsp chopped mint Juice of half a lemon 2 tbsp olive oil

■ Cut the panir into even-sized chunks about 2.5cm x 2.5cm (1 inch). Cut the capsicums into squares and the onion and tomatoes into large chunks, about the same size as the panir.

■ Thread the panir and vegetables onto 8 skewers (pre-soaked if using wooden ones), dividing the ingredients equally. Place in a shallow, non-metallic dish that will hold the skewers in a single layer.

■ Place all the remaining ingredients and half the oil into a bowl and mix until combined. Pour the marinade over the skewers, turning each skewer until the panir and vegetables are well coated with the marinade. Cover and refrigerate for 2 or 3 hours.

■ Remove the skewers from the fridge about half an hour before cooking and heat the grill or barbecue. Brush or spray the skewered ingredients with oil, and grill or barbecue on all sides for 3–4 minutes until the panir and vegetables are charred around the edges.

■ Serve hot with a spicy salad and nan or roti (chapatti).

SPRING ROLLS

Although the filling is a little different, Indian spring rolls are similar to Chinese spring rolls in appearance, texture and taste, only much spicier. This is quite an easy recipe that is even easier if you use ready-made spring roll pastry available from Asian grocers and supermarkets.

SERVES 4–6	**Filling**	50g (2 oz) cabbage, thinly sliced
Preparation and cooking time: 35–40 minutes	2 tbsp olive oil	50g (2 oz) panir, cut into small dice
	2 cloves of garlic, minced or finely chopped	1¹/₂ tbsp soy sauce
	Small piece of ginger, grated	**Pastry**
	(or a portion of prepared garlic and ginger mix, page 30, thawed)	100g (3 oz) plain flour
		50g (2 oz) cornflour
	1 carrot, grated	1 small egg, beaten
	1 green capsicum, cut into thin strips	Oil for deep-frying

■ Heat the oil in a karahi or saucepan and add the garlic and ginger. Stir-fry for a minute or two and add all the remaining ingredients for the filling except for the panir and soy sauce, and mix well.

■ Continue to stir-fry on medium heat for 5–6 minutes until the vegetables are tender crisp. Add a little water if required to prevent them from burning. Turn off the heat and stir in the panir and soy sauce. Allow the vegetables to cool while making the 'pastry'.

■ Sieve the flour and cornflour into a medium bowl; add the beaten egg and enough water to make a thickish batter. Do not over mix.

■ Heat a pancake pan, or non-stick frying pan, and brush or spray with a little oil. Pour in about 2 tablespoonfuls of batter and spread thinly over the pan to make a thin pancake. Turn when the underside is lightly brown and brown the other side. Repeat with the remaining batter.

■ Place a pancake on a flat surface in front of you. Put about a tablespoonful of vegetable filling onto the half nearest to you, about 2.5cm (1 inch) from the edge. Fold this edge over the filling, fold over once more, then bring in the sides. Continue to roll tightly until you have a neat roll. Secure with a toothpick if necessary.

■ Repeat with the remaining filling and pancakes.

■ Deep-fry the rolls in hot oil until crisp and golden. Drain and serve with a sauce of your choice. Tamarind Sauce (page 50) or the Coriander and Mint Drizzle (page 47) is delicious with these rolls.

ALOO KI TIKKI

A delicious snack any time of the day, Aloo Ki Tikki is a popular vegetarian entrée in Indian restaurants. It is a tasty, spicy potato tikki (patty), pan-fried until golden and crispy. Serve it with an assortment of chutneys and sweet, sour or spicy sauces.

There are as many recipes for making these lovely little potato cakes as there are cooks. The one below is quick and easy.

**SERVES 4–6
(MAKES 12 PATTIES)**

**Preparation and cooking time:
35–40 minutes**

225g (8 oz) potatoes, peeled and cut into large chunks
Knob of butter
3 tbsp frozen peas
1/2 onion, finely chopped
1 tsp salt
1 tsp turmeric

1 tsp ambchoor
2 green chillies, finely chopped (or half a portion of prepared chillies, page 30)
1 tbsp chopped coriander
1 tsp garam masala
Oil for pan frying

- Cook the potatoes in boiling salted water for about 15 minutes until tender. Drain well and return to the hot saucepan to dry off completely.

- Add the butter and mash the potato until smooth.

- Microwave or boil the peas until just cooked and add to the mashed potato with all the remaining ingredients except the oil. Mix well.

- Take about a tablespoonful of mixture and, with oiled hands, roll first into a ball and then flatten slightly to make a patty. Repeat with the remaining potato mixture.

- Heat a heavy-based, non-stick frying pan and pour in enough oil to cover the base. Add the potato patties to the pan in batches and cook over low to medium heat for about 5 minutes each side until golden and crisp. Add a little more oil as required.

- Serve hot with Kashmiri Chat (page 39), Mango Chutney (page 171) or Tamarind Sauce (page 50).

TIP
For a lower fat version, spray tikkies lightly with oil and bake in a hot oven (220°C, 425°F or gas mark 7) for 20–25 minutes.

DHAL SOUP

A simple example of 'fusion' cooking, this warming soup is simple to prepare and delicious to eat. You can use practically any combination of vegetables that are in season.

SERVES 6–8

Preparation and
cooking time:
1 hour 15 minutes

1 cob of sweetcorn
1 onion
1 medium potato
1 medium carrot
1 stick of celery
200g approx. (7 oz) butternut squash
2 ripe tomatoes, chopped
2 tbsp olive oil
1 tsp ground cumin

1 tsp ground coriander
1 tsp chilli powder
3 tbsp red lentils, washed
2 litres (70 fl oz/4.2 US pints) water
1 vegetable stock cube
2 tsp salt or to taste
Juice of a lime
1 tbsp chopped coriander

- Remove husk and hairs from the corn and discard. Using a sharp knife, slice off the kernels. Peel and coarsely chop the remaining vegetables.

- Place all the vegetables in the bowl of a food processor and process briefly, or chop finely.

- Heat the oil in a large heavy-based saucepan and add the spices. Fry for a few seconds and stir in the vegetables.

- Stir-fry for about 2 minutes and add the lentils, water, stock cube (crumbled) and salt. Bring to the boil. Turn down the heat and skim the froth off the surface.

- Partly cover and simmer for about an hour, stirring once or twice. Stir in the lime juice and coriander, and serve.

9. TANDOORI COOKING

W HO CAN possibly resist the delicious morsels of succulently tender meat and hot, puffy nan breads emerging from the flaming hot coals? With its origins in the north of India, the tandoor has taken permanent residence in the West!

Used widely throughout Asia and the Middle East, there is evidence that the tandoor has been around for a very long time and was used by ancient civilizations since before the birth of Christ. It is constructed from clay and has a unique shape; wide at the bottom and narrowing to about a third of its width at the top.

The somewhat pot-bellied shape of the tandoor is sometimes referred to disparagingly by Indians to describe someone roundly obese or 'tandoor-like'.

The heat from the red hot embers at the base of the tandoor is intensified by the narrowing shape and temperatures can reach as high as 480°C (896ºF). The intense heat cooks food quickly, crisping it on the outside while maintaining a tender succulence on the inside. Meat and fish are skewered on seekhs (long metal skewers) and cooked by lowering the seekhs into the oven from the top and leaving them in the hot interior for a few minutes, the hooked ends of the seekhs hanging from bars placed at the mouth of the tandoor; breads are cooked by slapping them onto the inside wall. The tandoor is traditionally fired with charcoal although some of the modern ovens use electricity or gas.

The tandoor shares some similarities with the Italian wood-fired oven, and the 'common' barbecue, but its shape and the cooking techniques employed in its use make it distinctly unique. The extremely hot temperatures, the charcoal that fires it and the flame-grilled flavour and crispness it imparts to cooked foods are difficult to replicate at home. Nevertheless good results can be achieved using a very hot oven, an effective griller or, if weather permits, a barbecue.

TANDOORI MARINADE

Apart from a tandoor, a good marinade and time are the key elements required for producing good 'tandoori' dishes.

Makes approximately 300ml (11 fl oz)
Preparation time: 5 minutes

275ml (10 fl oz) plain yogurt
2 green chillies, roughly chopped
2 tsp grated ginger
3 cloves of garlic
1 1/2 tsp salt
1 tsp red chilli powder
1 tsp black cumin
1 1/2 tsp garam masala
2 tsp vinegar
2 tbsp olive oil
1/2 tsp red food colouring or 2 tsp paprika
1/2 tsp yellow food colouring or 2 tsp turmeric

Combine the yogurt, green chillies, ginger and garlic in a blender until smooth.

Empty into a bowl and add all the remaining ingredients. Mix until well combined.

Tandoori dishes

Tandoori Chicken
Buy small birds no more than 1.2kg (2 lb 8 oz) in size. Divide into portions, skin and score the flesh. Marinate overnight for best results. Cook in a very hot oven for about 20 minutes or under a very hot grill, turning two or three times, for about 15 minutes. Works well on a barbecue too.

Chicken Tikka
The majority of restaurants use thigh fillets for this dish but you might like to try breast meat for a change. Marinate for a minimum of 6 hours or overnight for even better flavour. This is great cooked on the barbecue. Or you might like to put the chunks of meat onto skewers and cook under a very hot grill for 10–15 minutes until cooked through.

Lamb Tikka and Lamb Chops
The meat for Lamb Tikka needs to be tender and lean. Use meat from the leg, or try lamb fillets. Trim the fat from the lamb chops. Marinate the meat overnight for best results.

Tandoori Beef or Pork
Marinate diced pork fillet or rump steak overnight. Place onto skewers and cook under a hot grill or over a barbecue.

Seafood
Fish and prawns are delicious cooked in the 'tandoori' way. Use fish with firm flesh and green (uncooked) prawns if you can get them. Experiment with different varieties of fish such as trout or salmon; you really can't go too far wrong. Marinate seafood for 15–30 minutes only.

Panir
Marinated and grilled cubes of panir are delicious and nutritious if you prefer a vegetarian dish. Marinate for 2–3 hours, skewer and cook under a hot grill for a few minutes until crisp and golden. Alternate the pieces of panir with marinated vegetables for a change.

Vegetables
Mushrooms are a good 'meaty' vegetable and excellent done this way. Buy even-sized button mushrooms or the fuller flavoured field mushrooms. Wipe with a damp cloth (do not wash) and marinate for 3–4 hours. Baste with oil and cook under a very hot grill, turning once.

Serve your tandoori dishes sizzling (see page 42) with a sauce of your choice, a crisp green salad, rice and/or nan bread.

10.   CHICKEN DISHES

MEAT AND poultry are not generally consumed daily in India, with some populations existing happily on a varied and nutritious diet consisting exclusively of grains, lentils, beans, vegetables and dairy foods. Chicken is a popular choice for non-vegetarian meals and is served in a myriad of tantalizing ways according to the style of cooking of the region or the styles adopted by restaurant chefs to create varied and tasty dishes for the restaurant menu.

Most of the curries served in Indian restaurants are made using chicken prepared and pre-cooked every couple of days or so by the restaurant chef. Combined with a selection of spices, herbs and the curry sauce, they allow your meal to be served to you within minutes of you placing your order.

These preparation and cooking techniques, unique to restaurant cooking, also serve to differentiate the flavour and texture of Indian restaurant food from traditionally made dishes.

Using the method outlined here, you can pre-cook the chicken, refrigerate or freeze it, and, together with some curry sauce, prepare one or more of the delicious curry recipes detailed in the following pages within about 20–25 minutes.

PREPARING CHICKEN

Preparation and cooking time: 25 minutes.
For 6–8 people you will require:

5 large chicken breast fillets, preferably free range
    (approximately 900g/2 lb with skin and bone removed)
6 tbsp olive oil
1 tsp turmeric
4 tbsp reserved curry sauce, prepared to the end of stage 2,
    page 32

With a sharp knife remove all fat and sinew from the chicken fillets, rinse and pat dry with paper towels. Cut each fillet into 8 equal-sized pieces, about 2.5cm (1 inch). Place the oil, turmeric and curry sauce into a large saucepan and mix well. Cook on medium heat, stirring continuously, until the sauce starts to darken in colour (approximately 4–5 minutes).

Add the chicken and stir until all the pieces are well coated with the sauce. Turn down the heat, cover and continue cooking for 15–20 minutes, or until the chicken is tender, stirring frequently.

Remove the chicken pieces with a slotted spoon (leaving behind the sediment) and place them in a clean container.

Use immediately or cool and refrigerate for up to 4 days.

Freezing: Freeze for up to 2 months.

TIP
If you don't have any reserved curry sauce, use 2 tablespoonfuls of very finely chopped onion.

Chicken dishes menu

Chicken Methiwalla
Marinated chunks of chicken, grilled and braised in a tasty, peppery, sun-dried fenugreek masala base.

Chicken Yogurt Curry
Tender pieces of chicken breast, in a lightly tangy yogurt-based sauce, robustly spiced.

Moghlai Cashew Jhool
Mildly spiced, opulently rich with cashew nut paste and finished with cream.

Chicken and Chickpea Curry
A satisfying combination of tender chicken breast, chickpeas and mushrooms in a mildly spiced coconut milk sauce.

Chicken Chettinad
A stunning south Indian speciality with coconut and a fragrant blend of lightly roast spices, tomatoes and curry leaves.

Murgh Hariyali Masala
Tender breast pieces, marinated in fresh herbs, green chillies and spices. A fresh and flavoursome dish.

Chicken Tikka Masala
The all-time favourite, marinated chunks of chicken grilled and braised in a creamy sauce.

Parsi Chicken with Apricots
Boneless chicken stir-fried in an aromatic spice blend and simmered in a thick sauce with fresh fruity flavours.

Goan Coconut Chicken
Chicken pieces in a delicious, generously spiced, tamarind-flavoured creamy coconut sauce.

CHICKEN METHIWALLA

Methi is the Indian name for fenugreek leaves which have a distinctly aromatic 'curryish' aroma and flavour. This dish is inspired by northern India, where methi is used much like spinach in meat and vegetable curries and snacks. Unlike spinach, it adds a lot of very moreish flavour.

Fenugreek leaves can be purchased in bunches, much like coriander, from Indian grocers and greengrocers and are also easily grown (see page 18). Sun-dried methi is available in small packs and is generally of good quality. It can be used in place of fresh leaves if these are not available, but fresh is definitely best.

SERVES 4

Preparation and cooking time: 20–25 minutes

3 tbsp olive oil
1 bunch (about 150g/5 oz) fenugreek (methi) leaves, chopped (or 50g/2 oz dried methi)
425ml (15 fl oz) curry sauce (page 32)

1/2 tsp salt
1/2 tsp chilli powder
450g (1 lb) chicken fillets, pre-cooked as on page 59
1 tsp garam masala

■ Heat the oil in a large, heavy-based frying pan and add the fenugreek leaves. If using fresh leaves cook on low heat for about 10 minutes. If using dried leaves, stir in hot oil for a few seconds only.

■ Add the curry sauce, salt and chilli powder and bring to the boil. Cook on high heat for about 5 minutes until the sauce is thick and the oil floats to the surface.

■ Add the chicken and bring to the boil. Stir in the garam masala and simmer for about 5 minutes, stirring frequently. Serve.

CHICKEN YOGURT CURRY

This is a lovely creamy dish but without the calories of cream, combining a modified version of an authentic Indian food (the yogurt curry) with tender morsels of chicken. For best results use fresh home-made yogurt (page 24) or buy the freshest, best-quality plain yogurt you can find. No curry sauce is required for this dish.

SERVES 4

Preparation and cooking time: 30 minutes

250ml (9 fl oz) plain yogurt
1 tbsp gram flour (besan)
1 tsp salt
200ml (7 fl oz) cold water
2 tbsp olive oil
1 tsp black mustard seeds
1 tsp whole cumin seeds
1 onion, finely chopped
2 cloves of garlic

2.5cm (1 inch) piece of ginger
(or a portion of prepared garlic and ginger mix, page 30, thawed)
2 green chillies, finely chopped (or half a portion of prepared chillies, page 30)
1 tsp turmeric
450g (1 lb) chicken fillets, pre-cooked as on page 59
1 tsp garam masala
1 tbsp finely chopped coriander

■ In a large bowl, whisk together the yogurt, gram flour, salt and water. Heat the oil in a large, heavy-based saucepan, and add the mustard and cumin seeds. Fry for a few seconds on medium heat until they start to pop.

■ Add the onion and fry for about 5 minutes. Stir in the garlic, ginger and chillies and stir-fry for a couple of minutes longer.

■ Sprinkle on the turmeric, stir, and add the yogurt mixture. Bring to the boil stirring continuously and turn down the heat. Simmer, stirring frequently, for about 20 minutes.

■ Add the chicken and gently bring back to a simmer. Simmer for 5 minutes. Stir in the garam masala and coriander. Serve.

MOGHLAI CASHEW JHOOL

Dishes thickened with rich nut pastes were first introduced to India by the Moghuls who settled in the north of the country in 1525. The Moghul emperors brought with them opulence formerly unknown to the region. Money was no object to the extravagant settlers, and their imagination was boundless. Their favourite foods – almonds, cream and dried fruits – were lavishly incorporated into the traditional cuisine. This beautifully spiced, deliciously creamy dish reflects some of the grandeur of that bygone era.

SERVES 3–4

Preparation and cooking time: 20 minutes

3 tbsp olive oil
1/2 tsp ground cumin
1 tsp ground coriander
6 green cardamom pods, crushed
425ml (15 fl oz) curry sauce (page 32)
1 tsp Kashmiri chilli powder or 1/2 tsp chilli powder and 1/2 tsp paprika

1 tsp salt
4 tbsp thick cream
50g (2 oz) raw cashew nuts, processed until fine.
    Note: Ground almonds may be used instead of cashews.
450g (1 lb) chicken fillets, pre-cooked as on page 59

■ Heat the oil in a large, heavy-based frying pan and add the cumin, coriander and cardamom and fry for a few seconds. Add the curry sauce and bring to the boil.

■ Stir in the chilli powder, paprika if using, and salt. Simmer for about 5 minutes and stir in the cream and ground nuts.

■ Simmer for a further 5 minutes and stir in the chicken. Continue to cook on low heat for another 5 minutes, stirring often. Serve.

CHICKEN AND CHICKPEA CURRY

This delicious and unusual chicken curry (pictured on the cover) is thought to originate on the south-west coast of India. It has distinct Goan and south Indian influences. The chickpeas and mushrooms make this curry almost a 'one pot' dish that is tasty, satisfying and nutritious.

SERVES 4–6

Preparation and cooking time: 30 minutes

3 tbsp olive oil
1 tsp black mustard seeds
2 cloves of garlic, sliced
2.5cm (1 inch) piece of ginger, julienned
250g (9 oz) mushrooms, sliced thickly
4 bay leaves, roughly torn
2.5cm (1 inch) piece of cinnamon
4 cardamom pods, crushed
1 tsp ground coriander
1 tsp ground cumin

1/2 tsp chilli powder
1/2 tsp turmeric
400g (14 oz) can cooked chickpeas
425ml (15 fl oz) curry sauce, page 32
1/2 tsp paprika
1 tsp salt
450g (1 lb) chicken fillets, pre-cooked as on page 59
250ml (9 fl oz) coconut milk
1 red chilli, de-seeded and sliced
1 tbsp chopped coriander

- Heat the oil in a deep, heavy-based frying pan and add the mustard seeds. Shake the pan over the heat for a few seconds until the seeds start to pop, and add the garlic, ginger and mushrooms.

- Stir-fry for 3 minutes and add the bay leaves, cinnamon, cardamoms, coriander, cumin, chilli and turmeric. Fry for a minute and stir in the chickpeas, curry sauce, paprika and salt.

- Bring to the boil, and cook on high for 5 minutes until the sauce thickens. Add the chicken and coconut milk, bring back to the boil and simmer for 10 minutes.

- Stir through the red chilli and serve sprinkled with coriander.

CHICKEN CHETTINAD

Chettinad, a prosperous region in Tamil Nadu, southern India, is renowned for its spice concoctions. Historically a trading region, spices were one of the main commodities traded, possibly leading to the abundant use of spices in its cuisine. Hence, this recipe does require a number of different spices, but once you smell the beautiful aroma of the roasted spices, I think you will feel it's worth it. Fresh coconut will produce the best results, but dried, shredded (desiccated) coconut is fine.

SERVES 4

Preparation and
cooking time:
25–30 minutes

Spice mix
2 tsp olive oil
1 tsp poppy seeds
1/2 tsp fennel seeds
1/2 tsp coriander seeds
1/2 tsp black peppercorns
3–4 dried red chillies
2cm (just under 1 inch) piece of cinnamon, broken
    into small pieces
5 green cardamom pods
2 cloves
1 tbsp grated coconut (or desiccated coconut)

2 tbsp olive oil
4 curry leaves
1 ripe tomato, chopped
425ml (15 fl oz) curry sauce (page 32)
1/2 tsp salt
1/2 tsp chilli powder
1 tsp paprika
1/2 tsp turmeric
450g (1 lb) chicken fillets, pre-cooked as on page 59
4 cherry tomatoes, halved, or a large tomato sliced
    into eight pieces
Juice of half a lime
1 tbsp chopped coriander

■ Heat the oil in a small pan and roast the spices and coconut on low heat for about a minute until aromatic. Cool and grind to a fine powder in a pestle and mortar or electric grinder.

■ Heat the remaining oil in a large, heavy-based frying pan and add the curry leaves, stir for a few seconds and add the chopped tomato. Stir-fry for 3 or 4 minutes until pulpy and add the spice mix. Fry on low heat for about 5 minutes, until the mixture starts releasing the oil.

■ Add the curry sauce, salt, chilli powder, paprika and turmeric and bring to the boil. Simmer for about 5 minutes. The sauce will be quite thick because of the spice mix. Add a little water if required.

■ Add the chicken, bring back to a simmer and cook for 3 minutes. Stir in the tomatoes, lime juice and coriander, and serve.

MURGH HARIYALI MASALA

This is absolutely delicious and so simple and quick to prepare. It is essential to use fresh herbs though; they are the mainstay of this spectacular dish. Curry sauce is not required for this dish.

SERVES 3–4

Preparation and cooking time:
30 minutes (plus marinating time)

3 chicken fillets about 450g (1 lb) in weight
1 tsp salt
4 tbsp coriander leaves
4 tbsp mint leaves
4 fresh curry leaves
4 green garlic tops (optional)
4 spring onions
2–3 green chillies

2.5cm (1 inch) piece of ginger, roughly chopped
2 cloves of garlic, roughly chopped
1 tsp garam masala
6 tbsp yogurt
2 tbsp olive oil
3 tbsp thick cream
1 tsp gram flour (besan)
100ml (3 fl oz) hot water

■ Wash the chicken fillets, pat dry with paper towels, and cut into 2.5cm (1 inch) chunks. Place in a large bowl.

■ Put the salt, herbs, spring onions, chillies, ginger, garlic, garam masala, yogurt and 1 tablespoonful of the oil into the bowl of a blender or food processor and process to a paste.

■ Add the herb paste to the chicken, mix well and refrigerate for 2–3 hours or overnight.

- Remove from the fridge about half an hour before cooking and stir in the cream and gram flour.

- Heat a wide, heavy-based (preferably non-stick) frying pan and add the remaining oil. Add the chicken and all the marinade to the pan and stir-fry on high heat until the chicken is opaque.

- Turn down the heat a little, and continue to cook, stirring and turning the chicken pieces, until the sauce is quite dry at which stage it will release the oil, about 6–7 minutes.

- Continue cooking for a few minutes longer until the chicken pieces start to brown slightly. Now add the water and stir in to create a thick, creamy sauce.

- Simmer gently for 3 or 4 minutes. Add more water if you want a little more sauce.

- Serve.

Note: The gram flour is important as it prevents the sauce from spitting.

CHICKEN TIKKA MASALA

No Indian restaurant cookbook could be complete without a recipe for the famous Chicken Tikka Masala.

Chicken Tikka Masala is probably, more than any other restaurant dish, a hybrid of Indian and Western tastes: *tikka* is a morsel of roasted meat, traditionally eaten without curry sauce or 'gravy', a practice seemingly unattractive to Western palates. The 'masala' part of the dish is the Western touch that possibly came about in Glasgow in the 1960s when a long-suffering Indian chef mixed some spices and yogurt into canned tomato soup and presented his ever complaining customers with the sauce they demanded. The rest, as they say, is history.

With a few enhancements since that fateful time, the dish has become an icon of Indian restaurant cuisine. Indeed, in 2001, Britain's foreign minister Robin Cook declared it to be Britain's 'national dish' and the British consume vast amounts of it each week. It is, in fact, even more popular than Fish and Chips.

There are many recipes for Chicken Tikka Masala. This one is easy to prepare and quite delicious.

SERVES 3–4 Preparation and cooking time: 15 minutes	4 tbsp olive oil 1/2 tsp ground cumin 425ml (15 fl oz) curry sauce (page 32) 1 tsp paprika 1 tsp salt 1 level tsp chilli powder	Pinch of red food colouring (optional) 1 tsp garam masala 3 chicken fillets, freshly made into chicken tikka (page 58) 6 tbsp single cream 1 tbsp finely chopped coriander

■ Heat the oil in a large, deep frying pan, and stir in the cumin. Fry for a few seconds and add the curry sauce. Bring the sauce to the boil.

■ Add the paprika, salt, chilli powder and food colouring if using, and continue to cook on high heat, stirring frequently, for about 5 minutes or until the sauce thickens.

■ Turn down the heat and stir in the garam masala. Simmer for about 3 minutes.

■ Meanwhile, slice each piece of chicken tikka into two and add to the sauce. Stir in the cream and simmer for a further 2–3 minutes.

■ Serve sprinkled with the coriander.

TIP

If you have a little Tandoori Marinade (page 57) left over, stir a couple of teaspoonfuls of it into the sauce just before the cream. It adds extra colour and flavour.

Parsi Chicken with Apricots

This delicious Parsi dish has a lovely balance of sweet and sour flavours derived from juicy apricots, soft brown sugar and vinegar. Lamb can be used instead of chicken for a change.

SERVES 4

Preparation and cooking time: 20–25 minutes

2 tbsp olive oil
2 tsp tomato paste (tomato purée double concentrate)
1/2 tsp turmeric
425ml (15 fl oz) curry sauce (page 32)
1/2 tsp salt
1 tsp chilli powder
1 tsp paprika

6 dried apricots, quartered
1 tsp soft brown sugar
1 tbsp vinegar
450g (1 lb) chicken fillets, pre-cooked as on page 59
1 tbsp thick cream
1 tsp garam masala
1 tbsp chopped coriander

■ Heat the oil in a large, heavy-based frying pan and add the tomato paste and turmeric. Stir-fry for a minute.

■ Add the curry sauce, salt, chilli powder, paprika, apricots, sugar and vinegar. Bring to the boil and simmer for 5 minutes.

■ Stir in the chicken , bring back to the boil and simmer, stirring often, for 5 minutes.

■ Stir in the cream and garam masala. Simmer for a minute. Serve sprinkled with coriander.

GOAN COCONUT CHICKEN

Nowhere is the Portuguese influence more evident than in the delicious and colourful cuisine of Goa. Although seafood and rice are the staples, this chicken recipe encompasses all that is good about Goan food. It has lots of tasty sauce to eat with rice and bread.

SERVES 4

Preparation and cooking time: 20–25 minutes

Spice mix
1/2 tsp fennel seeds
1/2 tsp fenugreek seeds
1/2 tsp black peppercorns
1 tsp coriander seeds
1 tsp cumin seeds
4 green cardamoms
4 cloves
2.5cm (1 inch) piece of cinnamon

3 tbsp olive oil
1/2 tsp turmeric
325ml (12 fl oz) curry sauce (page 32)
1 tsp salt
1 tsp chilli powder
1 tsp paprika
300ml (11 fl oz) coconut cream
450g (1 lb) chicken fillets, pre-cooked as on page 59
2 tsp tamarind paste dissolved in 2 tbsp warm water

■ Grind all the spices for the spice mix to a fine powder in a pestle and mortar or electric grinder.

■ Heat the oil in a large, heavy-based frying pan and add the spice mix. Fry on medium heat for about a minute until aromatic.

■ Stir in the turmeric, curry sauce, salt, chilli powder and paprika. Bring to the boil and cook on high heat for about 3 minutes until thickened slightly. Turn down the heat.

■ Add the coconut cream and bring slowly to a simmer. Add the chicken to the sauce and mix well. Simmer for about 5 minutes.

■ Stir in the tamarind and serve.

11. LAMB DISHES

THROUGHOUT its long history, India has been invaded by foreign armies of traders and settlers from all over the world, beginning with the Greeks, led by Alexander the Great, as far back as 326 BC, followed by many others from various destinations over the ages. The culinary influence of Greek, Middle Eastern, Portuguese and English invaders is clearly evident in Indian cuisine.

The rich and opulent Moghul settlers of the sixteenth century introduced meat dishes to the Indian nation whose people had existed well for centuries on grains, pulses, nuts, fruits and dairy products. Although goat is the preferred meat for the non-Muslim population, lamb is widely consumed throughout India.

Pre-cooked lamb pieces are always at the ready in the restaurant fridge to be combined with various herbs and spices according to the dish that is being prepared. Tender, good quality meat is essential for most of the curries served in Indian restaurants, the tougher cuts being reserved for any traditional, slow-cooked dishes that may be on the menu.

Leg of lamb is the cut of choice for the majority of restaurant curries. Get your butcher to remove the bone and trim the fat and gristle from the meat. Cut the remaining lean meat into 2.5cm (1 inch) cubes and prepare as shown here. If you wish to use cuts with the bone in, increase the quantities accordingly.

Note: The meat has a tendency to dry out when refrigerated. Spoon some of the oil left in the pan onto the meat, coating each piece to keep it moist.

PRE-COOKED LAMB

Serves 6–8

900g (2 lb) boned, diced lamb
8 tbsp vegetable oil
1 tsp turmeric
4 tbsp reserved curry sauce, prepared to the end of step 2 (page 32)

Wash the meat and pat dry with paper towels. Place the oil, turmeric and curry sauce in a large saucepan and mix well. Cook on medium heat, stirring continuously until the sauce begins to darken in colour (4–5 minutes).

Add the meat and stir until all the pieces are well coated. Turn down the heat and cook, covered, for 30–40 minutes or until the meat is tender. Add a little water to prevent the meat from sticking to the bottom of the pan and burning, and stir frequently.

Remove the lamb pieces using a slotted spoon, leaving behind the sediment, and place in a clean container.

Use immediately, or cool and refrigerate for up to 4 days.

Freezing: Freeze for up to 2 months.

Lamb dishes menu

Parsi Lamb Curry
Boned, diced leg of lamb simmered in a tangy, aromatic spice mixture with garlic, ginger and tomatoes, served with crispy potato straws.

Lamb Kalia
Tender diced lamb and crisp potato chunks, in a lightly spiced sauce.

Bhindi Ghost
Lamb and Okra Curry. A fragrant mix of fresh okra, diced lamb and roast spices in a tasty masala base.

Tamatar Ghost
Boneless diced lamb, braised with vine-ripened tomatoes, fresh herbs and spices.

Badami Lamb Pasanda
Marinated, tender strips of lamb fillet in a mildly spiced, lusciously creamy and aromatically flavoursome sauce.

Kali Mirch Ka Ghost
Tender lamb pieces simmered in a spicy sauce flavoured with gently roasted black peppercorns.

Moghul Lamb with Turnips
Succulent pieces of lamb, in a rich dark sauce with sweet, juicy turnips. Inspired by the decadent Moghul era.

Rogan Josh
Tender pieces of lamb in a delicious thick sauce flavoured with an aromatic spice blend. An old favourite.

PARSI LAMB CURRY

The unique fruity, spicy flavours of this dish are inspired by the Parsi style of cooking, which, in turn, is a combination of Gujerati and Iranian cuisine. The crispy fried potato straws, *sali*, add a lovely crunch to the dish.

SERVES 4 Preparation and cooking time: 20–25 minutes	3 tbsp olive oil 2.5cm (1 inch) stick of cinnamon 4 cardamom pods 6 curry leaves 1 tbsp tomato paste (tomato purée double concentrate) 425ml (15 fl oz) curry sauce (page 32) 1 tbsp vinegar	2 tsp soft brown sugar 1 tsp chilli powder 1/2 tsp turmeric 1/2 tsp salt 450g (1 lb) pre-cooked lamb (page 71) 1 tsp garam masala 1 tbsp chopped coriander Sali, to serve (optional)

■ Heat the oil in a deep, heavy-based frying pan and add the cinnamon, cardamoms and curry leaves. Stir for a few seconds and add the tomato paste. Stir-fry for about a minute.

■ Stir in the curry sauce, vinegar, sugar, chilli powder, turmeric and salt and bring to the boil. Cook the sauce on high heat for about 3 minutes until thickened slightly.

■ Add the lamb to the sauce and bring back to the boil. Stir in the garam masala and simmer gently for 5 minutes. Stir in the coriander and ladle into a serving dish.

■ Sprinkle on the sali if using and serve.

SALI
(CRISPY POTATO STRAWS)

Grate or julienne 2 large peeled potatoes and soak in salted, chilled water for a few minutes.

Drain the potato well and spread on a tea towel until dry.

Deep-fry potato in hot oil until golden brown. Drain and serve with Parsi Lamb Curry.

LAMB KALIA

This dish of tender lamb and fried potatoes is based on the Kashmiri dish 'Kalia'. Traditionally made with mutton marinated in yogurt and ginger to tenderize it followed by long simmering, the restaurant version is, by comparison, quick and easy to prepare. Sometimes fried cauliflower is also added to the dish with the potatoes.

SERVES 4

Preparation and cooking time: 25–30 minutes

2 medium-sized potatoes, peeled
1 tsp salt, plus a little extra
4 tbsp olive oil
1 onion, sliced
2.5cm (1 inch) piece of ginger, grated
2 cloves of garlic, finely chopped
  (or a portion of prepared garlic and ginger mix, page 30, thawed)
200ml (7 fl oz) plain yogurt

1 tsp chilli powder
1/2 tsp paprika
1/2 tsp turmeric
1 tsp ground coriander
400ml (14 fl oz) curry sauce (page 32)
450g (1 lb) pre-cooked lamb (page 71)
1/2 tsp garam masala
2 tbsp chopped coriander

- Cut the potatoes into approximately 2.5cm (1 inch) chunks and cook in boiling, salted water for about 5 minutes or until just tender. Drain well and sprinkle lightly with a little salt.

- While the potatoes are boiling, heat 1 tablespoonful of the oil in a heavy-based frying pan and fry the onion slices until lightly browned. Set aside.

- Combine the ginger, garlic, yogurt, chilli powder, paprika, turmeric, salt and coriander in a small bowl.

■ Heat 2 tablespoonfuls of the oil in the same pan used for the onions and add the yogurt mixture. Stir-fry for 3 minutes and add the curry sauce. Bring to the boil and simmer for 10 minutes until the sauce is thick and the oil rises to the surface.

■ Meanwhile, heat the remaining oil in another frying pan and fry the potato on medium heat, turning until all sides are golden.

■ Add the meat to the yogurt and curry sauce mixture and bring back to the boil. Add the garam masala and simmer for 5 minutes.

■ Stir half the potato chunks and half the coriander into the onion mixture. Reheat for a minute. Serve sprinkled with the remaining crispy potato chunks and remaining coriander.

BHINDI GHOST

The bhindi, also called okra or ladies' fingers, add an extra dimension to this dish by helping to thicken and flavour the sauce. Be careful not to cook the bhindi for more than the specified time as they have a tendency to become slimy. It is important to wash and dry the bhindi before slicing them for the same reason.

SERVES 4–5

Preparation and cooking time: 25–30 minutes

Spice mix
8 black peppercorns
3 cloves
1 tsp cumin seeds
1 tsp coriander seeds
4 green cardamom pods

250g (9 oz) bhindi (okra)
3 tbsp olive oil
2.5cm (1 inch) piece of ginger, finely chopped
2 cloves of garlic, finely chopped
   (or a portion of prepared garlic and ginger mix,
   page 30, thawed)

2 green chillies, finely chopped
 (or half a portion of prepared chilli, page 30)
2 ripe tomatoes, chopped
1 tsp salt
1 tsp turmeric
1/2 tsp chilli powder
525ml (18 fl oz) curry sauce (page 32)
450g (1 lb) pre-cooked lamb (page 71)
1/2 tsp garam masala
1 tbsp chopped coriander

■ In a small dry pan, roast the peppercorns, cloves, cumin, coriander and cardamoms for about 2 minutes over medium heat. Remove the spices from the hot pan as soon as they become aromatic. Cool and grind in a pestle and mortar or electric grinder.

- Meanwhile, wash the bhindi whole, drain well and pat dry with paper towels or a clean tea towel until quite dry. Slice into 5cm (2 inch) pieces.

- Heat the oil in a deep, heavy-based frying pan and fry the ginger and garlic for about a minute. Add the green chillies and fry for another minute.

- Stir in the tomatoes, salt and turmeric and cook over low heat for a few minutes until the tomatoes are soft and pulpy.

- Add the bhindi to the pan, sprinkle on the chilli powder and roast spices. Stir-fry on medium heat for 4 or 5 minutes.

- Add the curry sauce and bring to the boil, cook on medium heat for about 5 minutes, stirring frequently, until thickened.

- Add the meat, bring back to the boil and simmer for a further 5 minutes. Stir through the garam masala and coriander, and serve.

TAMATAR GHOST

Fresh ripe tomatoes add colour, freshness and flavour to this simple lamb curry. Good quality, flavoursome tomatoes are a must for a really tasty dish.

SERVES 4

Preparation and cooking time: 25–30 minutes

3 tbsp olive oil
1 tsp ground cumin
2 tsp ground coriander
2 ripe tomatoes, chopped
1/2 tsp salt
1/2 tsp turmeric
1/2 tsp chilli powder

425ml (15 fl oz) curry sauce (page 32)
450g (1 lb) pre-cooked lamb (page 71)
1/2 tsp garam masala
1/2 tsp dried ground methi (fenugreek) leaves
6 cherry tomatoes, halved
2 tbsp chopped coriander

■ Heat the oil in a deep, heavy-based frying pan and add the cumin and coriander. Stir-fry for a few seconds and add the tomatoes, salt, turmeric and chilli powder.

■ Stir-fry on high heat for a couple of minutes then turn down the heat and simmer the tomatoes on low heat, stirring frequently, until the mixture is pulpy, a dark red and releasing the oil. This will take about 10 minutes.

■ Add the curry sauce and bring to the boil. Boil on high for about 5 minutes until the sauce has thickened.

■ Stir in the lamb and bring back to the boil. Add the garam masala and methi, and simmer for 5 minutes.

■ Stir through the cherry tomatoes and half the coriander. Heat for about a minute.

■ Serve sprinkled with the remaining coriander.

BADAMI LAMB PASANDA

Pasanda is a popular north Indian and Pakistani dish with its origins in the royal courts of the Moghul emperors. It is a deliciously fragrant and satisfying dish that is usually made with lamb but can be made with any meat, vegetable or with panir. The lamb fillets used in this recipe cook really quickly and are beautifully tender, but leg meat works just as well with longer cooking.

SERVES 4

Preparation and cooking time: 30 minutes (plus marinating time of 15–30 minutes)

500g (1 lb 2 oz) lamb fillets
2 cloves of garlic, minced or finely chopped
Small piece of ginger, grated
(or a portion of prepared garlic and ginger mix, page 30, thawed)
2 green chillies, finely chopped
(or half a portion of prepared chilli, page 30)
1 tbsp finely chopped mint leaves
3 tbsp plain yogurt
2 tbsp olive oil

1 tsp ground coriander
1/2 tsp ground cumin
1/2 tsp turmeric
425ml (15 fl oz) curry sauce (page 32)
1 tsp salt
1/2 tsp paprika
4 tbsp single cream
1 tbsp ground almonds
1/2 tsp garam masala
1 tbsp rosewater (optional)

■ Trim the lamb fillets, and using a meat mallet, or rolling pin, flatten until just over 0.5cm (1/4 inch) thick. Cut into slices about 3.5cm (11/2 inches) long and just over 1cm (1/2 inch) wide.

■ Combine the garlic, ginger, chilli, mint and yogurt in a medium bowl and add the meat. Stir well to coat the meat slices with the marinade. Leave to marinate for 15–30 minutes.

■ Heat the oil in a deep, heavy-based frying pan and carefully (it will splutter) add the meat and marinade. Stir-fry for about 3 minutes on medium-high heat or until most of the liquid evaporates.

■ Add the coriander, cumin and turmeric and stir-fry for a minute. Stir in the curry sauce and salt and bring to the boil. Turn down the heat and simmer for 10 minutes, stirring often, until the sauce thickens.

■ Stir in the paprika, cream and ground almonds and simmer for a further 5 minutes, stirring regularly. Add the garam masala and heat through for a minute.

■ Remove from the heat and stir in the rosewater if using. Serve.

KALI MIRCH KA GHOST

This dish of tender lamb pieces has a delicious peppery bite to it. Use whole black peppercorns, crushed, and don't be tempted to use ground black pepper.

SERVES 4

Preparation and cooking time: 15–20 minutes

1 tsp whole black peppercorns, crushed
3 tbsp olive oil
2 tsp ground coriander
1 tbsp tomato paste (tomato purée double concentrate)
1/2 tsp turmeric

425ml (15 fl oz) curry sauce (page 32)
1/2 tsp salt
450g (1 lb) pre-cooked lamb (page 71)
4 whole green chillies, slit lengthways
1/2 tsp garam masala
2 tbsp chopped coriander

■ Dry-roast the peppercorns in a small pan over medium heat for a minute or two until aromatic. Remove from the pan and set aside.

■ Heat the oil in a deep, heavy-based frying pan and add the ground coriander. Stir-fry for a few seconds and stir in the tomato paste and turmeric.

■ Cook on medium heat for 2 minutes and add the curry sauce and salt. Bring to the boil and cook on high heat, stirring often, until the sauce is really thick and the oil rises to the surface. This will take about 4–5 minutes.

■ Add the lamb, roasted peppercorns and chillies. Bring back to the boil, stir in the garam masala and simmer gently, stirring often, for 5 minutes to allow the meat to absorb the flavours. Stir in half the coriander.

■ Serve sprinkled with the remaining coriander.

MOGHUL LAMB WITH TURNIPS

The Moghuls didn't do anything by halves and this dish is testament to that, a dish that in times of old would have been served in the royal palaces. Richly spiced, but not chilli-hot, this is a dish to make when young, sweet turnips are in season.

If you can, use larger lamb pieces as prepared for balti meat (page 90) for more authenticity.

SERVES 4

Preparation and cooking time: 25–30 minutes

3 tbsp olive oil
2 tsp ground coriander
1 tsp ground cumin
3 green cardamom pods, crushed
1 tbsp tomato paste (tomato purée double concentrate)
1/2 tsp turmeric
2 green chillies, finely chopped (or a half portion of prepared chilli, page 30)

250g (9 oz) turnips, cut into chunks
425ml (15 fl oz) curry sauce (page 32)
1 tsp paprika
1 tsp salt
500g (1 lb 2 oz) pre-cooked lamb (page 71) or prepared as for balti meat (page 90)
1/2 tsp garam masala
1 tbsp thick cream

■ Heat the oil in a deep, heavy-based frying pan and add the coriander, cumin and cardamom. Stir-fry for a few seconds and add the tomato paste, turmeric and green chillies.

■ Fry for 1 minute and stir in the turnips. Stir-fry on medium heat for 2 minutes and add the curry sauce, paprika and salt. Bring to the boil and simmer for 10 minutes.

■ Add the lamb and bring back to the boil and simmer again for 8–10 minutes or until the turnips are tender, the sauce has almost completely reduced and the oil has separated from the sauce.

■ Stir in the garam masala and cream, and cook for a minute longer. Serve.

ROGAN JOSH

Although there is a recipe for Rogan Josh in *The Curry Secret*, it is such an old favourite I thought it is worth repeating here for those readers who don't have a copy of the original book. I have made some alterations to the original recipe in keeping with changing tastes and demands.

SERVES 4

Preparation and cooking time: 15–20 minutes

3 tbsp olive oil
2.5cm (1 inch) stick of cinnamon
3 cloves
4 green cardamom pods
1 tsp ground coriander
$1/2$ tsp ground cumin
425ml (15 fl oz) curry sauce (page 32)

2 tsp paprika
1 tsp chilli powder
$1/2$ tsp salt
450g (1 lb) pre-cooked lamb (page 71)
$1/2$ tsp garam masala
4 tbsp plain yogurt
1 tbsp chopped coriander

■ Heat the oil in a deep, heavy-based frying pan and add the cinnamon stick, cloves, cardamoms, coriander and cumin. Stir-fry for a few seconds.

■ Add the curry sauce, paprika, chilli powder and salt, and bring to the boil. Continue to cook on high heat stirring often, for about 5 minutes or until the sauce has thickened.

■ Add the meat and bring back to the boil. Turn down the heat and add the garam masala. Simmer for 5 minutes.

■ Stir in the yogurt, 1 tablespoonful at a time, waiting until each addition is completely incorporated before adding the next. Simmer and continue stirring for a minute after all the yogurt has been added.

■ Serve sprinkled with the coriander.

12. BALTI DISHES

SELL the sizzle not the steak? In the case of these dishes, it may be more accurate to say sell the sizzle *before* the steak.

First you hear the sizzle, an instant later the delicious aroma arouses your senses and tickles your tastebuds as you wait in anticipation for the dish making its way to your table. And it does not disappoint. Generous quantities of succulent meats, tasty vegetables, fresh herbs and spices combined with thick flavoursome sauces make these dishes quite memorable.

The origins of the dish can be traced back several centuries to a place called Baltistan, an area now located in the far north of Pakistan. It was introduced to England in the 1960s with the opening of the first 'Balti House' in Birmingham. The freshly cooked, wonderfully aromatic, gently spiced curries were such a hit with the British that within a few years hundreds of balti houses sprung up all over the UK. Balti refers to the people of Baltistan, the origins of the dish and the wok-like utensil in which it is served.

The Indian *balti* (utensil), also known as *karahi*, and the Chinese wok are very much the same in shape and structure, though which came first is impossible to determine. China had long had an association with India through its trading routes with the inevitable influences on the two ancient cultures and their cuisines. The influence of the spicy dishes of Szechuan is subtly evident in the balti curry.

In terms of Indian restaurant cooking, the balti and karahi essentially started life as the same thing, though the dishes they now represent have evolved to take on slightly differing characteristics. The balti dishes retain their original concept and favour more subtle combinations and flavours while the karahi dishes have been designed to deliver a more authentic taste with stronger spice and herb mixes.

To get the sizzle that is synonymous with these dishes, heat your balti or karahi until very hot and carefully (it will splutter and splash) transfer the simmering curry into it. Serve immediately.

Balti curries menu

Balti Chicken
A sumptuous dish with succulent chicken pieces, stir-fried with whole spices, tomatoes, capsicums and onions, served sizzling.

Balti Fish
Fish pieces, served in the balti style, subtly spiced in a delicious creamy sauce.

Balti Subzi
A delicious combination of cauliflower, carrots, capsicums, potatoes and fresh coriander.

Balti Meat
Tender pieces of lamb, beef or goat meat in a thick, tasty sauce with spices, capsicums, onions and tomatoes.

BALTI CHICKEN

This is a popular dish dating back to the original Balti Houses in Birmingham. I have used chicken breast fillets in this recipe, but you can use chicken portions on the bone if you wish for a more traditional dish. Allow an extra 15 minutes or so cooking time for chicken on the bone.

SERVES 4

Preparation and cooking time: 30 minutes

3–4 chicken fillets (about 500g or 1 lb 2 oz)
4 tbsp olive oil
2–3 green garlic tops, chopped (optional)
1/2 tsp cumin seeds
1/2 tsp ground cumin
1 tsp ground coriander
2.5 cm (1 inch) stick of cinnamon
4 green cardamoms
1/2 tsp turmeric

425ml (15 fl oz) curry sauce (page 32)
1 tsp salt
1/2 tsp chilli powder
1/2 tsp paprika
1 medium-sized onion
1 green capsicum
1 tomato
1/2 tsp garam masala
1 tbsp chopped coriander

■ Wash the chicken fillets and pat dry with paper towels. Trim off fat and sinew and slice each fillet into 4 pieces.

■ Heat 3 tablespoonfuls of the oil in a large, deep frying pan, add the chopped garlic tops if using and stir-fry for 3 or 4 minutes.

■ Add the cumin, coriander, cinnamon, cardamoms and turmeric. Stir for a few seconds until aromatic and add the chicken pieces.

■ Stir-fry the chicken for about 5 minutes on medium to high heat and add the curry sauce, salt, chilli powder and paprika. Bring to the boil, stir and turn down the heat. Leave to simmer for about 15 minutes, stirring now and again.

■ Meanwhile, peel and quarter the onion. Slice each quarter into two. Slice the capsicum in half and de-seed. Cut into approximately 2.5cm (1 inch) squares. Quarter the tomato.

■ Heat the remaining oil in a clean pan and add the onion and capsicum. Stir-fry on high heat for 3 or 4 minutes until the onion just starts to colour at the edges. Add the tomato and stir.

■ Add the onion, capsicum and tomato to the chicken and sprinkle on the garam masala. Continue to simmer for another 5 minutes or so, by which time the sauce should be thick and the oil should be separating on top of the sauce.

■ While the chicken is simmering, heat balti dishes on medium heat for about a minute. Carefully, spoon the hot curry into the dishes, sprinkle on the coriander and serve.

Balti Fish

Use any firm fish, including salmon if you like. King prawns are fantastic for this dish, or try a combination of seafood.

SERVES 4	500g (1 lb 2 oz) fish fillets or king prawns	1 tsp salt
Preparation and cooking time: 20–25 minutes	3 tbsp olive oil	$1/2$ tsp paprika
	$1/2$ tsp turmeric	1 medium-sized onion
	$1/2$ tsp chilli powder	1 green capsicum
	2 spring onions, chopped	1 tomato
	$1/2$ tsp ground cumin	$1/2$ tsp garam masala
	$1/2$ tsp ground coriander	Juice of half a lemon
	425ml (15 fl oz) curry sauce (page 32)	1 tbsp chopped coriander

■ Wash the fish fillets or prawns (shell and de-vein if using whole prawns). Pat dry with paper towels. Cut the fish into large chunks about 5cm (2 inches) in size.

■ Place the fish with about a tablespoonful of the oil in a bowl. Sprinkle on a little of the turmeric and chilli powder, and cover while preparing the sauce.

■ Heat 1 tablespoonful of the oil in a large, deep frying pan, add the spring onions and stir-fry for 2 minutes.

- Add the cumin, coriander and remaining turmeric. Stir for a few seconds until aromatic and add the curry sauce, salt, remaining chilli powder and paprika. Bring to the boil, stir and turn down the heat. Leave the sauce to simmer and reduce for about 10 minutes, stirring now and again.

- Meanwhile, peel and quarter the onion. Slice each quarter into two. Slice the capsicum in half and de-seed. Cut into approximately 2.5cm (1 inch) squares. Quarter the tomato.

- Heat the remaining oil in a clean pan and add the onion and capsicum. Stir-fry on high heat for 3 or 4 minutes until the onion just starts to colour at the edges. Add the tomato and stir.

- Stir the onion, capsicum and tomato into the sauce with the garam masala. Simmer.

- Wipe clean and heat the pan used to fry the vegetables. Add the fish chunks or prawns to the pan and cook on medium to high heat until beginning to colour. Sprinkle on the lemon juice.

- Add the fish to the sauce and vegetables and stir through carefully to avoid breaking the fish pieces. Simmer until the fish is cooked through, about 5 minutes. Fish will flake easily when it is cooked, prawns will be opaque.

- Meanwhile heat balti dishes on medium heat for about a minute. Carefully, spoon the curry into the dishes, sprinkle on the coriander and serve with rice and breads.

BALTI SUBZI

This recipe uses a combination of cauliflower, carrots, capsicums and potatoes but you can use a combination of peas, mushrooms, green beans, aubergine, cabbage or any other vegetables that are in season and at their best.

SERVES 4–6

Preparation and cooking time: 30–35 minutes

225g approx. (8 oz) fresh cauliflower florets
1 large potato, peeled and cut into large chunks
2 carrots, peeled and diced
4 tbsp olive oil
2 spring onions, chopped
2–3 green garlic tops (optional)
1 small green capsicum, de-seeded and cut into squares
1 small red capsicum, de-seeded and cut into squares

$^1/_2$ tsp ground cumin
$^1/_2$ tsp ground coriander
$^1/_2$ tsp turmeric
2 ripe tomatoes, cut into small dice
300ml (11 fl oz) curry sauce (page 32)
1 tsp salt
$^1/_2$ tsp chilli powder
$^1/_2$ tsp garam masala
2 tbsp chopped coriander

■ Boil or steam the cauliflower, potato and carrots until almost tender.

■ Meanwhile, heat the oil in a large, deep frying pan, add the spring onions and garlic tops if using, and stir-fry for 2 or 3 minutes. Add the capsicums and stir-fry for a further 2 or 3 minutes.

■ Stir in the cumin, coriander and turmeric. Stir for a few seconds until aromatic and add the tomatoes. Stir-fry for a minute or two until the tomatoes are pulpy. Stir in the pre-cooked cauliflower, carrots and potato.

■ Add the curry sauce to the vegetables with the salt and chilli powder. Bring to the boil.

■ Turn down the heat and simmer the vegetables on low heat for about 15 minutes until the liquid has almost evaporated. There should just be a thick sauce clinging to the vegetables.

■ Stir in the garam masala and half of the fresh coriander into the curry.

■ Heat balti dishes on medium heat for about a minute. Carefully, spoon the curry into the dishes, sprinkle on the remaining coriander and serve.

BALTI MEAT

Traditionally, fresh goat, beef or lamb used for balti curries would be simmered over low fires for several hours. Obviously this is not practical for restaurant cuisine, and apart from chicken fillets and fish, which cook in minutes, the meat for the balti dish below needs to be pre-prepared to the stage when, with the addition of a few spices and fresh herbs, you can have a delicious and authentic balti curry ready in minutes. Prepare the meat as indicated for lamb curries (page 71), but cut it into larger chunks.

You can use any meat of your choice. Lamb is the preferred meat in most Indian restaurants, but the dish works just as well with beef or goat.

SERVES 4		
Preparation and cooking time: 20–25 minutes	4 tbsp olive oil 2–3 green garlic tops, chopped (optional) $1/2$ tsp ground cumin 1 tsp ground coriander $1/2$ tsp turmeric 500g (1 lb 2 oz) lamb or other meat prepared as on page 71 500ml (18 fl oz/1 US pint) curry sauce (page 32)	1 tsp salt $1/2$ tsp chilli powder $1/2$ tsp paprika 1 medium-sized onion 1 green capsicum 1 tomato $1/2$ tsp garam masala 1 tbsp chopped coriander

■ Heat 1 tablespoonful of the oil in a large, deep frying pan, add the chopped garlic tops if using and stir-fry for 3 or 4 minutes. Add the cumin, coriander and turmeric. Stir for a few seconds until aromatic and add the cooked meat.

■ Stir-fry for a minute or so and add the curry sauce, salt, chilli powder and paprika. Bring to the boil, stir and turn down the heat. Leave to simmer for about 15 minutes, stirring now and again.

■ Meanwhile, peel and quarter the onion. Slice each quarter into two. Slice the capsicum in half and de-seed. Cut into approximately 2.5cm (1 inch) squares. Quarter the tomato.

■ Heat the remaining oil in a clean pan and add the onion and capsicum. Stir-fry on high heat for 3 or 4 minutes until the onion just starts to colour at the edges. Add the tomato and stir.

■ Add the onion, capsicum and tomato to the meat and sprinkle on the garam masala. Continue to simmer for another 5 minutes or so, by which time the sauce should be thick and the oil should be separating on top of the sauce.

■ While the meat is simmering, heat balti dishes on medium heat for about a minute. Carefully, spoon the hot curry into the dishes, sprinkle on the coriander and serve.

13. KARAHI AND OTHER TRADITIONAL DISHES

P OPULAR restaurant dishes like Chicken Tikka Masala evolved from modifications of traditional dishes adapted to be gentler on unsuspecting Western tastebuds. As the Western palate has become accustomed to Indian cuisine, tastes have changed and there is now a significant demand for more pungent flavours. To satisfy this demand, Indian restaurants are serving more authentic dishes. This chapter shows you how to make some of the most popular of these dishes with the same ease and convenience as the other restaurant curries.

KAHARI DISHES

The Indian *karahi* is the same utensil as the *balti*, however the karahi curries served in Indian restaurants are spicier adaptations of the traditional balti dishes. These and the other traditional dishes in this section are wonderful if you are a 'curry tragic' who loves the robust flavour of Indian spice and herb combinations.

KARAHI CURRIES MENU

KARAHI SUBZI
A mix of fresh seasonal vegetables in a dry, spicy and aromatic sauce.

KARAHI CHICKEN
Pieces of chicken on the bone, cooked with ginger, garlic and chillies in a thick, spicy sauce served sizzling.

KARAHI KEEMA
Minced lamb, richly flavoured with ginger, garlic and chillies.

KARAHI MEAT
Generous pieces of lamb on the bone in a rich, pungently aromatic and spicy sauce.

Karahi Subzi

You can use whatever vegetables are in season for this dish. I have used aubergines cooked with onions. This delicious recipe is generous with the oil as aubergines do soak it up but it makes them lovely and silky.

SERVES 4–6

Preparation and cooking time: 30 minutes

6 small long aubergines (approx. 350g or 12 oz)
6 tbsp of olive oil
2 cloves of garlic, finely chopped
2.5cm (1 inch) piece of ginger, finely chopped
  (or a portion of prepared garlic and ginger mix,
  page 30, thawed)
3 green chillies, finely sliced (or a portion of prepared
  chilli, page 30)
2 large onions, sliced
6 spring onions, white part only

1 tsp fennel seeds
1 tsp cumin seeds
1 tsp fenugreek seeds
1 tsp onion seeds
1 tsp turmeric
1 tsp chilli powder
2 tsp salt
150ml (5 fl oz) curry sauce (page 32)
6 cherry tomatoes (optional)
1 tsp garam masala

■ Wash and wipe the aubergines. Slice in half and cut each half into 2 slices.

■ Heat the oil in a karahi or large, heavy-based frying pan and add the garlic, ginger and chillies. Fry for a minute.

■ Add the aubergine and onions to the pan and stir-fry on high heat until the vegetables begin to brown, about 5 minutes.

■ Pull the vegetables towards the edges of the pan and let the oil pool in the middle. Place all the seeds into the hot oil and stir them around for a minute or two on medium heat, and then stir them into the vegetables.

■ Sprinkle over the turmeric, chilli powder and salt, and cook for a minute longer before stirring in the curry sauce.

■ Bring to the boil, turn down the heat and simmer for about 5 minutes, stirring now and again. Add the tomatoes if using and simmer for a further 5 minutes. Stir through the garam masala and cook for a minute more.

■ Meanwhile heat karahi dishes for about a minute on medium to high heat. Carefully transfer the curry to the hot karahis and serve sizzling.

KARAHI CHICKEN

Traditionally, the bone is left in providing extra flavour and richness to the sauce, but chicken fillets can be used instead. You can also use the chicken prepared as for chicken curries (page 59) to speed up the preparation, but, if you have time, it is worth trying this dish the traditional way.

SERVES 6–8

Preparation and cooking time:
Step 1:
45 minutes
(30 minutes if using fillets)

Step 1, preparing the chicken
1 chicken approx. 1.8kg (4 lb), preferably free-range
2 tbsp olive oil
1 red onion, finely sliced
2 cloves of garlic, ground to a paste
2.5cm (1 inch) piece of ginger, ground to a paste
 (or a portion of prepared garlic and ginger mix, page 30, thawed)

2 green chillies, finely chopped (or a portion of prepared chillies, page 30)
2 tsp salt
2 ripe tomatoes, chopped

■ Have your butcher skin the chicken, separate the wings and drumsticks and chop the rest of the chicken into 8 pieces. Rinse the chicken portions well and drain.

■ Heat the oil in a large, heavy-based saucepan and add the onion. Stir around for a minute or two and add the garlic, ginger and chillies. Stir-fry for 2 or 3 minutes until aromatic.

■ Add the chicken and stir to coat in the oil, and add the salt and tomatoes. Stir-fry until sizzling. Stir in 2 tablespoonfuls of water.

■ Turn down the heat and simmer, covered, for about 30 minutes (10–15 minutes if using sliced chicken fillets), stirring occasionally until the chicken is just cooked through and most of the liquid has evaporated.

■ Use immediately or cool and refrigerate or freeze for later use.

Preparation and cooking time: Step 2: 20–25 minutes	**Step 2, preparing the curry** 2 tbsp olive oil 1 tsp turmeric 2 tsp garam masala	1–2 tsp chilli powder to taste 500ml (18 fl oz/1 US pint) curry sauce (page 32) 2 tbsp chopped coriander

■ Heat the oil in a large, heavy-based frying pan or saucepan, and add the turmeric, half the garam masala and the chilli powder. Cook, while stirring, for a minute or so until aromatic.

■ Add the cooked chicken and juices and stir to coat in the spices. Once it is bubbling, turn down the heat and simmer, covered, for about 10 minutes, stirring frequently to allow the chicken to absorb the flavours. There should be very little liquid at this stage so that everything is gently frying in the oil.

■ Add the curry sauce and bring back to the boil. Turn down the heat and simmer for another 8–10 minutes until the sauce is thick and the oil separates to the top. Stir in the remaining garam masala and half the coriander.

■ Meanwhile, heat karahi dishes for about a minute on medium heat, carefully pour in the curry, sprinkle with the remaining coriander and serve.

KARAHI KEEMA

Similar to 'Keema Peas' but spicier, this is a delicious dish eaten with chapattis, spiced yogurt and *achar* (pickles).

SERVES 4–5

Preparation and cooking time:
Step 1:
45 minutes

Step 1, preparing the meat
2 tbsp olive oil
2 red onions, sliced
500g (1 lb 2 oz) lean minced lamb

1^1/$_2$ tsp salt
1 tsp turmeric
1 can (400g or 14 oz) of chopped tomatoes

- Heat the oil in a large, heavy-based saucepan, and add the onions. Stir around for 2 or 3 minutes over high heat and add the meat.

- Stir-fry the meat and onions over high heat, breaking up any lumps, until the meat changes colour, about 3 or 4 minutes. Turn down the heat, stir in the salt, turmeric and tomatoes.

- Bring to the boil and turn down the heat. Simmer, uncovered, over low heat for about 30–35 minutes, stirring now and again, until all the liquid has evaporated.

- Use immediately or cool and refrigerate, or freeze for later use.

Preparation and cooking time:
Step 2:
15–20 minutes

Step 2, preparing the curry
2 tbsp olive oil
6 curry leaves (optional)
4 cloves of garlic, ground to a paste
2.5cm (1 inch) piece of ginger, ground to a paste
   (or a portion of prepared garlic and ginger mix,
   page 30, thawed)
2 tsp julienned ginger (optional)

2 green chillies, finely chopped (or half a portion of
   prepared chillies, page 30, thawed)
1 tsp ground cumin
1 tsp paprika
1 tsp chilli powder
250ml (9 fl oz) curry sauce (page 32)
200g (7 oz) frozen peas
1 tsp garam masala

■ Heat the oil in a large, heavy-based frying pan and add the curry leaves if using, and fry for a few seconds.

■ Add the garlic, ginger, chillies and cumin, and stir-fry for a couple of minutes until aromatic. Stir in the paprika and chilli powder.

■ Add the meat to the pan and stir-fry until sizzling. Stir in the curry sauce and bring to the boil. Add the peas and bring to the boil again.

■ Turn down the heat and simmer for 10–15 minutes until quite dry. Stir in the garam masala and cook for a minute to allow the meat to absorb the spices.

■ Meanwhile heat karahi dishes for a minute on medium to high heat and carefully ladle in the meat. Serve.

Karahi Meat

Shoulder of lamb is superb for this recipe because it lends itself to long, slow cooking after which the meat is deliciously spiced and tender and almost falling off the bone. You can use leg of lamb cut into 5cm (2 inch) chunks if you prefer.

SERVES 4–6

Preparation and cooking time:
Step 1:
2–2¹/2 hours

Step 1, preparing the meat

1kg (2 lb 4 oz) lamb shoulder, cut into large pieces
2 tbsp olive oil
2 red onions, finely sliced
2 cloves of garlic, ground to a paste
2.5cm (1 inch) piece of ginger, ground to a paste (or a portion of prepared garlic and ginger mix, page 30, thawed)

2 green chillies, finely chopped (or a portion of prepared chillies, page 30)
2 tsp salt
2 ripe tomatoes, chopped

- Rinse the meat, drain well and pat dry with paper towels (wet meat will not brown).

- Heat the oil in a large, heavy-based saucepan and add the onions. Stir around for a minute or two on high heat and add the lamb pieces. Stir around in the hot oil until the meat colours, about 5 minutes.

- Add the garlic, ginger and chillies to the meat, stir-fry for a minute or two and add the salt. Stir and turn down the heat. Cook covered, stirring occasionally, for 1 hour.

- Stir in the tomatoes and cook for another 45 minutes to an hour until the meat is tender and a rich dark brown.

- Skim off any excess fat, use immediately or cool and refrigerate, or freeze for later use.

Preparation and cooking time: Step 2: 30 minutes	**Step 2, preparing the curry** 2 tbsp olive oil 1 tsp ground cumin 2 tsp turmeric 2 tsp garam masala 1–2 tsp chilli powder to taste	1 tbsp tomato paste (tomato purée double concentrate) 1 tsp dried ground methi (fenugreek) leaves 500ml (18 fl oz) curry sauce (page 32) 2 tbsp chopped coriander

■ Heat the oil in a large, heavy-based frying pan or saucepan, and add the cumin, turmeric, half the garam masala, chilli powder and tomato paste.

■ Cook, stirring, for a few seconds, then add the cooked meat and juices and stir to coat in the spices.

■ Once it is bubbling, turn down the heat and simmer, covered, for about 10 minutes, stirring now and again to allow the meat to absorb the flavours. There should be very little liquid so that everything is gently frying in an oily masala. Sprinkle on the methi.

■ Add the curry sauce and bring back to the boil. Turn down the heat and simmer for 8–10 minutes until the sauce is thick and the oil begins to separate.

■ Stir in the remaining garam masala and half the coriander.

■ Meanwhile, heat karahi dishes for about a minute on medium to high heat, carefully pour in the curry, sprinkle with the remaining coriander and serve.

Other traditional dishes menu

Dhal Makhani
A deliciously earthy, creamy dhal of mixed lentils and pulses flavoured with ginger, garlic and onions.

Chicken Jhol
Chicken pieces cooked with a traditional mix of onions, garlic and ginger and spiced with mustard seeds, cloves, cinnamon and pepper, and a touch of vinegar.

Dhesi Chicken
Punjabi fare with succulent pieces of chicken, onions, ginger, garlic, chillies and fresh herbs. A superb balance of authentic tastes in a delicious sauce.

Dhesi Style Saag
A traditional dish, this is a mix of greens, simmered until tender, puréed and flavoured with ginger, garlic and chillies.

Dhaba Style Lamb Curry
Lamb Punjabi style. Boneless lamb in a rich, thick sauce flavoured with lamb bones, onions, ginger, garlic, green chillies and fresh herbs.

Yogurt Curry
A tangy, hot and flavoursome mix of potatoes, onions, whole spices and fresh and dried herbs simmered in a yogurt sauce thickened with gram flour.

Achari Ghost
Lamb simmered in pickling spices – fennel, onion and mustard seeds – a dish with delicious and robust flavours.

Punjabi Cabbage
From the rich terrain of northern India, freshly sliced cabbage stir-fried with whole cumin, ginger and spices.

Shikari Ghost
Lamb with bone in, cooked in the traditional way of the Indian hunters.

DHAL MAKHANI

For something so simple, this is quite a sumptuous dish – thick, creamy and satisfying. You can use 100 per cent urad dhal or a mix of dhals (pulses) as I have. Traditionally made with generous amounts of ghee and makhan (home-made butter), this recipe uses olive oil and a little cream.

SERVES 4–6

Preparation and cooking time: 2 hours (or 30 minutes if using a pressure cooker)

150g (5 oz) urad dhal (black gram)
50g (2 oz) moong dhal
50g (2 oz) yellow split chana
1 litre (35 fl oz/2.1 US pints) cold water
4 tbsp olive oil
1 small onion, finely chopped
2 cloves of garlic, finely chopped
2.5cm (1 inch) piece of ginger, finely chopped (or a portion of prepared garlic and ginger mix, page 30, thawed)

2 green chillies, finely chopped (or half a portion of prepared chillies, page 30)
1 tsp dried ground methi (fenugreek) leaves (optional)
2 tsp salt
1 tsp garam masala
1 tbsp chopped coriander
2 tbsp thick cream

■ Mix all three dhals in a bowl and wash well. Drain and place the dhals in a large, heavy-based saucepan and add the water.

■ Bring to the boil, turn down the heat and cover the pan. Simmer gently for about 2 hours, stirring now and then, until the mixture is thick and creamy, adding a little more water if required. Or bring the pressure cooker to maximum pressure and cook for about 25 minutes.

Note: The dhal can be cooled and refrigerated at this stage for later use. It will keep well in the fridge for up to 3 days.

■ Meanwhile, heat the oil in a frying pan or small saucepan and fry the onion until beginning to brown at the edges.

■ Add the garlic, ginger and chillies and fry for a couple of minutes until aromatic. Stir in the methi if using.

■ Add the onion mixture, salt, garam masala and coriander to the dhal and mix well. Simmer for a minute.

■ Stir in the cream and serve.

Dhesi Style Saag

Panir, lamb, chicken and potato dishes made with saag (puréed spinach) are popular in Indian restaurants, but saag is rarely if ever served on its own. The tinned, puréed spinach used in restaurants is convenient and quite good when incorporated into other flavoursome ingredients, but it does not compare with the saag made with fresh leafy greens that is cooked in Indian households and eaten as a dish in its own right with cornmeal rotis (chapattis), yogurt and pickles. Meat and vegetarian dishes made with this saag are superb.

It is time-consuming to make but you can cook a large batch and freeze it in serving-size portions ready to use whenever you wish. You will need a large saucepan for this.

SERVES 8–10

Preparation and cooking time: 3 hours 30 minutes (or 1 hour 30 minutes if using a pressure cooker)

400g (14 oz) spring greens, mustard greens or purple sprouting broccoli
1 bunch of spinach (approx. 400g or 14 oz)
250g (9 oz) Brussels sprouts
1 large head of broccoli (approx. 300g or 11 oz)
1.5 litres approx. (40 fl oz/3.2 US pints) cold water
3 tsp salt

4 cloves of garlic, ground to a paste (or a portion of prepared garlic and ginger mix, page 30, thawed)
5cm (2 inch) piece of ginger, ground to a paste
2–3 green chillies, finely chopped (or a portion of prepared chillies, page 30)
150g (5 oz) cornmeal (fine polenta)

■ Wash the greens and spinach two or three times in plenty of cold water to remove all grit and soil, and drain. Remove any tough stalks from the spinach. Remove the outer leaves of the Brussels sprouts and rinse well. Rinse the broccoli.

■ Shred the greens and spinach, roughly chop the sprouts and broccoli, or process in a food processor until roughly chopped, and place in a saucepan.

■ Add the water and salt and bring to the boil. If using a pressure cooker, cook on maximum pressure for 45 minutes. Otherwise simmer, uncovered, for about 30 minutes (it has a tendency to boil over if covered in the early stages), stirring now and again.

- Once the mixture has settled down, cover the saucepan and simmer for 2 hours 30 minutes. Stir every half hour or so and add a little more water if the mixture dries out.

- There should only be enough water left at the end of the cooking to make the mixture into a thickish purée.

- Keeping the saucepan on the heat, stir in the garlic, ginger and chillies followed by the polenta and continue to cook for 4–5 minutes. Turn off the heat.

- The mixture now needs to be turned into a coarse purée. As the greens will be very soft, it is possible to purée them by stirring vigorously with a large wooden spoon. If you have a hand blender, it is even easier. Insert the blender into the mixture, switch on briefly. Move the blender about in the pan until all the mixture is puréed. Don't worry if it is a little 'sloppy' as the saag will thicken on cooling.

- Cool the saag, divide into portions and freeze if desired.

Note: If you can't buy spring greens, mustard greens or purple sprouting broccoli, increase the quantities of the other ingredients or try silver beet, kale or cabbage.

DHABA STYLE LAMB CURRY

Dhaba is the Indian word for a Punjabi family restaurant. The Dhaba curry is the basic traditional non-vegetarian curry of north India and is usually made with goat meat. It includes diced meat simmered until meltingly tender along with pieces of bone. Diners can be seen enthusiastically sucking on the bones at these *Dhabas*. I have provided the traditional recipe which requires some lamb pieces with bone left in, but you can use meat cooked as for lamb curries (page 71) along with some lamb or beef stock if you want to save time.

SERVES 6	**Step 1, preparing the meat**	
	2 tbsp olive oil	2 red onions, sliced
Preparation and cooking time:	500g (1 lb 2 oz) leg of lamb with bone in, cut into approx. 5cm (2 inch) pieces	2 tsp salt
Step 1:		1 can (400g or 14 oz) of chopped tomatoes
1 hour 30 minutes–	450g (1 lb) boned leg of lamb, cut slightly larger than	
1 hour 45 minutes	2.5cm (1 inch) chunks	

■ Heat half the oil in a large, heavy-based saucepan and add half the meat. Stir-fry until brown. Remove and repeat with the remainder of the meat.

■ Return the browned meat to the pan and add the onions. Stir-fry on high heat for about 5 minutes. Turn down the heat, mix in the salt and add the tomatoes. Bring to the boil, cover the pan and simmer on low heat for about 1 hour and 15 minutes or until the meat is tender and the onions have dissolved.

■ Use immediately or cool and refrigerate, or freeze for later use.

Preparation and cooking time:	**Step 2, preparing the curry**	
	2 tbsp olive oil	1 tsp chilli powder
Step 2:	4 cloves of garlic	1/2 tsp turmeric
20–25 minutes	5cm (2 inch) piece of ginger	1 tsp cumin powder
	(or 2 portions of prepared garlic and ginger mix, page 30, thawed)	1 tsp coriander powder
		2 tsp ground ginger
	2 green chillies, finely chopped	1 tsp paprika
	(or half a portion of prepared green chillies, page 30)	425ml (15 fl oz) curry sauce (page 32)
		2 tsp garam masala

■ Heat the oil in a large, heavy-based saucepan and add the garlic, ginger and chillies. Stir-fry for a minute and add the remaining spices except the paprika and garam masala, mix well and stir-fry for a minute.

■ Add the cooked meat and juices and stir well to coat with spices. Stir-fry on medium to high heat for about 5 minutes. Cover and allow the meat to simmer in the spices for 5–6 minutes on very low heat.

■ Add the paprika and the curry sauce and bring to the boil. Simmer, uncovered, for 10 minutes. Stir in the garam masala and serve.

Yogurt Curry

It may be hard to imagine a curry made from yogurt, but this is in fact quite a substantial (and incredibly tasty) dish popular throughout India. In more recent times it has been making an appearance in Indian restaurants, though generally as a 'sauce' with chicken, fish or vegetables. Try it with rice or chapattis; it is quite delicious and simple to make.

If you can, leave the yogurt out of the fridge overnight to sour slightly. You won't need to use any lemon juice if you do that.

SERVES 4–6

Preparation and cooking time: 1 hour

350ml (13 fl oz) plain yogurt
3 tbsp gram flour (besan)
2 tsp salt
700ml (25 fl oz/1¹/₂ US pints) cold water
3 tbsp olive oil
1 tsp fenugreek seeds
1 tsp whole black peppercorns
1 tsp whole cumin seeds
6 curry leaves (optional)
1 onion, sliced
4 spring onions, chopped
4 green garlic tops, chopped (optional)

2 cloves of garlic
2.5cm (1 inch) piece of ginger
   (or a portion of prepared garlic and ginger mix, page 30, thawed)
2 green chillies, finely chopped (or half a portion of prepared chillies, page 30)
2 tsp turmeric
1 potato, cut into chunks
4 whole green chillies
1 tsp garam masala
2 tbsp chopped coriander
Juice of half a lemon

- In a large bowl, whisk together the yogurt, gram flour, salt and water.

- Heat the oil in a large, heavy-based saucepan, and add the fenugreek seeds, peppercorns, cumin seeds and curry leaves if using. Fry for a few seconds until the seeds start to pop.

- Add the onion, spring onions and garlic tops if using, and fry on medium heat for 3 minutes. Stir in the garlic, ginger and chillies, and stir-fry for a couple of minutes.

- Stir in the turmeric and add the potato and whole chillies. Stir around for a minute and pour in the yogurt mixture. Bring to the boil and simmer over low heat for about 30–35 minutes, stirring frequently, until the potato is cooked through.

- Stir in the garam masala, coriander and lemon juice if using. Serve with rice or roti (chapatti).

TIP

For a variation, add onion, *palak* (spinach) or Vegetable Pakoras (page 46) to the finished yogurt curry.

ACHARI GHOST

Strong and spicy flavours are the keynotes of this dish. It is traditionally made with mutton simmered long and slow, but this recipe uses pre-cooked lamb, making it a quick and simple dish.

SERVES 4

Preparation and cooking time: 20–25 minutes

3 tbsp olive oil
4 whole red chillies
1 tsp cumin seeds
1/2 tsp black mustard seeds
1/2 tsp onion seeds
1/2 tsp fenugreek seeds
1/2 tsp fennel seeds

1/2 tsp turmeric
1 tsp chilli powder
4 tbsp plain yogurt
425ml (15 fl oz) curry sauce (page 32)
1/2 tsp salt
450g (1 lb) lamb cooked as on page 71

- Heat the oil in a large, heavy-based frying pan and stir in the chillies and all the spice seeds. Cook for a few seconds on high heat until the seeds start to pop, and add the turmeric and chilli powder.

- Stir in the yogurt and continue to stir on high heat for a minute or two until the yogurt bubbles and reduces.

- Add the curry sauce and salt, bring to the boil and stir in the cooked lamb.

- Turn down the heat and simmer for 10–15 minutes until the sauce is thick and the oil separates to the surface.

- Serve simmering hot with plain boiled rice.

PUNJABI CABBAGE

Fresh and spicy, this dish is a favourite in northern India. An excellent accompaniment to rich meat curries, yogurt and rotis (chapattis), it is simple to make and delicious served hot or cold. Make sure you use good quality fresh cabbage.

SERVES 4–6

Preparation and cooking time: 30 minutes

4 tbsp olive oil
1 small onion, sliced
1 tsp cumin seeds
2 cloves of garlic, finely chopped
2.5cm (1 inch) piece of ginger, finely chopped
  (or a portion of prepared garlic and ginger mix, page
    30, thawed)

2 green chillies, finely chopped (or a portion of
  prepared chillies, page 30)
1 tsp turmeric
500g (1 lb 2 oz) cabbage, sliced
1$^{1}/_{2}$ tsp salt
1 tsp garam masala

■ Heat the oil in a large, heavy-based frying pan or wok and add the onion. Fry, while stirring, for a few minutes, until the onion is transparent.

■ Stir in the cumin seeds and fry for a minute. Add the garlic, ginger and chillies, and stir-fry for a minute or two until aromatic.

■ Stir in the turmeric, followed by the cabbage. Stir-fry the cabbage on medium to high heat for 2 or 3 minutes and add in about 2 tablespoonfuls of water and the salt.

■ Turn down the heat a little and cook the cabbage for another 15 minutes, stirring frequently and adding a little more water if required to prevent it catching to the bottom of the pan.

■ Stir in the garam masala and serve.

SHIKARI GHOST

Shikari is the Indian word for hunter and this easy-to-cook dish from the Raj era is based on the cooking style of the *shikaris* when on a hunt. In its simplest form it is large pieces of fresh meat, rubbed with lime juice and hot spices, browned in ghee and simmered in salt and water until tender. The restaurant version includes some onion based sauce and fresh herbs.

Cook this dish on a day when you have some time to potter around the kitchen because, although it is simple to make, the meat takes a bit of time to cook and it does not freeze well.

SERVES 6–8	**Step 1, preparing the meat**	2 tbsp lime juice
	1 tsp cumin seeds	3 tbsp olive oil
Preparation and cooking time:	1 tsp coriander seeds	1 tsp ground ginger
Step 1:	1 tsp cardamom	2 tsp chilli powder
2–2½ hours	1 tsp cloves	400ml (14 fl oz) boiling water
	2.5cm (1 inch) stick of cinnamon	2 tsp salt
	1kg (2 lb 4 oz) lamb shoulder, cut into large pieces	

■ Grind the whole spices to a fine powder in an electric grinder or with a pestle and mortar.

■ Rinse the meat and drain well. Add the lime juice, 1 tablespoonful of the oil and all the spices, and using your hands rub well into the meat. Allow to stand for about 10 minutes.

■ Heat another tablespoonful of oil in a large, heavy-based saucepan and add half the meat. Stir-fry on high heat until well browned. Remove from the pan and repeat with the remaining oil and meat.

■ Return all the meat to the pan, add the water and salt and bring to the boil. Simmer, stirring occasionally, for about 2 hours until the meat is tender. Most of the liquid should have evaporated.

■ Skim off excess fat, use immediately or cool and refrigerate for up to 24 hours. For best results, do not freeze as the lovely spice flavours dull with freezing.

Preparation and cooking time:	**Step 2, preparing the curry**	950ml (33 fl oz/2 US pints) curry sauce (page 32)
30 minutes	1 tbsp olive oil	1 tsp chopped coriander

■ Heat the oil in a large, heavy-based frying pan and stir in the curry sauce. Bring to the boil and add the meat and juices.

■ Simmer gently for 15–20 minutes until the sauce is very thick. Stir in the coriander and serve.

14. PORK AND BEEF DISHES

I N THE HINDU WORLD of 900 million followers the cow is sacred; a divine creature to be esteemed and revered, not butchered and eaten. Even some of the Muslim kings who ruled India in long ago times prohibited their subjects from eating beef as it was considered offensive to the Hindus. Later, the newly emerging Sikh religion adopted the Hindu belief on the same basis and Sikhs too regard the cow as holy.

Mahatma Gandhi once wrote: '*If someone were to ask me what the most important outward manifestation of Hinduism was, I would suggest that it was the idea of cow protection.*'

From a source of milk to a provider of labour and religious inspiration, cows have played a pivotal role in the Indian way of life for many centuries. Indeed, in India a citizen can be sent to jail for killing or injuring a cow.

There are also religious restrictions on the consumption of pork. Islamic dietary laws forbid the eating of pork, believing it to be 'unclean', a harbinger of a multitude of diseases and a degrader of the character, morality and spirituality of the consumer.

There are, nevertheless, states in India that breed, sell and eat both pork and beef. Goa and Kerala on the west coast, supported by a high level of religious tolerance, readily consume pork and beef cooked in traditional vindaloos and bafaths as well as in European-style dishes.

Throughout the West, Seekhs and Hindus consume pork and pork products and Muslims beef. Understandably, Indian restaurants in the West generally have few, if any, pork or beef dishes on the menu. Here are a few traditional and tasty dishes to try at home.

PREPARATION OF MEAT FOR BEEF CURRIES

Tougher cuts of meat require longer cooking but are tastier. I suggest using braising or stewing steak for these recipes but you can use rump if desired.

2 tbsp olive oil
1 kg (2 lb 4 oz) braising beef cut into approx. 5cm (2 inch) pieces
2 onions, sliced
2 tsp salt

Heat half the oil in a large, heavy-based saucepan and add half the meat. Stir-fry until brown. Remove and repeat with the remainder of the meat.

Return the browned meat to the pan and add the onions. Stir-fry on high heat for about five minutes. Turn down the heat and stir in the salt.

Cover the pan with a tight-fitting lid and simmer on low heat for about 1^1/$_2$ hours or until the meat is tender and the onions have dissolved.

Use immediately or cool and refrigerate, or freeze for later use.

Beef dishes menu

Massaman Curry
Slow-cooked chunks of beef in a rich creamy sauce, mildly spiced.

Beef Vindaloo
The fabulously fiery flavours of the old Portuguese settlement of Goa. Hot and tangy, this dish is a delicious balance of pungent and aromatic spices.

Bombay Beef
Street food of Bombay, this combination of diced beef and potatoes is cooked in a sauce enriched with coconut milk and flavoured with spices.

Beef Badami
Mild beef curry with tender chunks of meat combined with aromatic spices and almonds finished with a touch of cream.

MASSAMAN CURRY

This is a dish more common in Thai restaurants, but I've included it because it originated with the Muslim community in India and because it is absolutely delicious. Unlike neighbouring countries, Thailand managed to remain free from colonization by European powers and, as a result, its food has limited outside influences. The Thais have, however, borrowed cooking styles from other countries such as China, India and Malaysia, and Massaman Curry is a stunning example of this.

Massaman curry paste is readily available from supermarkets and Asian grocers and is relatively good. If you would like to go a step better, I have included the recipe so you can make your own.

SERVES 4		
Preparation and cooking time: 30 minutes	2 tbsp olive oil 2 tsp grated ginger 1/2 tsp ground cumin 4 tbsp Massaman paste 6 green cardamom pods, crushed 2.5cm (1 inch) stick of cinnamon 100g (3 oz) peanuts	500ml (18 fl oz/1 US pint) coconut cream 500ml (18 fl oz/1 US pint) coconut milk 1 tbsp palm sugar or soft brown sugar 3 tbsp fish sauce 2 tsp tamarind paste dissolved in 2 tbsp warm water 450g (1 lb) pre-cooked beef (page 111)

MAKE YOUR OWN MASSAMAN PASTE

12 dried chillies, seeded and soaked
1 whole garlic bulb, cloves peeled
60g (2 oz) sliced shallots
1 tbsp ground coriander
1 tsp ground cumin
1 tsp ground pepper
1 tsp lemongrass, chopped
2.5cm (1 inch) piece of galangal, peeled, chopped
1 tsp kaffir lime zest
1 tbsp scraped, chopped coriander roots
3 tsp salt
1 tsp shrimp paste (belacan)
2 tbsp olive oil

Grind or process all the ingredients until you have a fairly smooth paste. Place in a clean jar, pour a little oil over the top and keep in the fridge for up to a week.

■ Heat the oil in a wok or heavy-based saucepan and add the ginger and cumin. Stir-fry for a few seconds and add the Massaman paste, cardamoms, cinnamon and peanuts. Stir-fry for 2 minutes.

■ Stir in half the coconut cream and bring to a simmer. Cook on medium heat, stirring often, until the cream is completely absorbed into the paste and the oil starts to separate from the mixture. Repeat with the remaining coconut cream.

■ Stir in the coconut milk and bring to a simmer. Simmer, stirring often, for about 10 minutes until the sauce has reduced.

■ Stir in the sugar, fish sauce, tamarind and meat. Bring back to simmer and cook on low heat for a further 10 minutes. Do not boil vigorously as the coconut sauce may separate.

■ Serve with boiled rice and rotis (chapattis).

BEEF VINDALOO

Vindaloo is the Portuguese name for vinegar and garlic. Perhaps it should be vinegar and chilli because vindaloo is notorious for being hot, hot, hot, and for some the hotter the better. However, for a good vindaloo, the heat should be balanced with other spicy flavours.

Traditionally, a combination of clear and dark vinegars is often used to make vindaloo. The clear vinegar is made from coconut and the dark from molasses. Balsamic vinegar works well.

SERVES 4	
Preparation and cooking time: 20 minutes	

4 cloves of garlic, finely chopped
2.5cm (1 inch) piece of ginger, grated or julienned
2 green chillies, finely sliced (or half a portion of prepared chilli, page 30)
1 1/2 tsp garam masala
1/2 tsp turmeric
1 tsp chilli powder or to taste

2 tbsp dark balsamic vinegar
3 tbsp olive oil
425ml (15 fl oz) curry sauce (page 32)
1/2 tsp salt
450g (1 lb) pre-cooked beef (page 111)
1/2 tsp dried ground methi (fenugreek) leaves (optional)

■ In a small bowl, mix together the garlic, ginger, chillies, 1 teaspoonful of the garam masala, turmeric, chilli powder and vinegar.

■ Heat the oil in a deep, heavy-based frying pan and add the spice mix. Stir-fry for about a minute or until aromatic.

■ Add the curry sauce and salt and bring to the boil. Cook on high for about 5 minutes until thickened.

■ Add the meat and bring back to a simmer. Stir in the remainder of the garam masala and methi if using. Simmer for 5 minutes or until the oil separates from the sauce.

■ Serve.

Bombay Beef

From the streets of Bombay comes this delicious combination of tender beef and potato in a beautifully spiced sauce made silky smooth by the addition of a little coconut milk. If you don't have coconut milk in the pantry, evaporated light milk or a little cream works well.

SERVES 4

Preparation and cooking time: 20 minutes

1 large or 2 small potatoes, peeled and cut into chunks
3 tbsp olive oil
2 tsp tomato paste (tomato purée double concentrate)
$1/2$ tsp turmeric
425ml (15 fl oz) curry sauce (page 32)

450g (1 lb) pre-cooked beef (page 111)
$1/2$ tsp salt
1 tsp chilli powder
4 tbsp coconut milk
1 tsp garam masala
1 tsp tamarind dissolved in 1 tbsp warm water

- Cook the potato in boiling salted water for about 10 minutes until just tender. Drain.

- Meanwhile, heat the oil in a deep, heavy-based frying pan and stir in the tomato paste and turmeric. Stir around in the hot oil for 10 seconds and add the curry sauce.

- Bring to the boil and cook on high for about 5 minutes until the sauce is thick and starting to release the oil.

- Stir in the beef, salt, chilli powder, cooked potato and coconut milk. Bring back to the boil and simmer gently for about 10 minutes, stirring often.

- Add the garam masala and tamarind, simmer for a minute, and serve.

BEEF BADAMI

A mildly spiced but flavoursome dish, Beef Badami is inspired by rich Moghul influences. The ground almonds and cream make for a deliciously creamy sauce while the lightly toasted flaked almonds add a contrasting crunch. A tasty and impressive dish fit for a king.

SERVES 4

Preparation and cooking time: 20–25 minutes

2 tbsp olive oil
4 cardamom pods
2.5cm (1 inch) stick of cinnamon
3 cloves
1/2 tsp ground cumin
1 tsp ground coriander
425ml (15 fl oz) curry sauce (page 32)

1/2 tsp salt
1/2 tsp chilli powder
450g (1 lb) pre-cooked beef (page 111)
30g (1 oz) almonds, ground to a fine powder
150ml (5 fl oz) single cream
1 tbsp flaked toasted almonds

■ Heat the oil in a deep, heavy-based frying pan and add the cardamom, cinnamon and cloves. Stir-fry on medium heat for a minute, add the cumin and coriander, and fry for a few seconds more.

■ Add the curry sauce, salt and chilli powder, and bring to the boil. Cook on high heat, stirring, for about 5 minutes until the sauce thickens.

■ Stir in the beef and almonds. Bring back to the boil and simmer for 5 or 6 minutes, stirring often. Add the cream and simmer for a further 3 minutes.

■ Serve sprinkled with the flaked almonds.

Pork dishes menu

Pork Tikka
Marinated chunks of pork fillet, encrusted with toasty spices on the outside and tender and juicy on the inside.

Mangalorean Style Pork Bafath
Boneless pork in an aromatic mix of roasted spices, south Indian style.

Pork and Sprouts
A tasty combination of tender pork fillet and fresh Brussels sprouts simmered in a spicy sauce until they melt in the mouth.

Chilli Pork
Juicy strips of pork with green and red chillies in a tangy flavoursome sauce.

PORK TIKKA

Another Punjabi delicacy regularly enjoyed at the Punjabi roadside restaurants, or *Dhabas*, this dish has little in common with the chicken dish of the same name. It is robustly spiced, though not too hot, very easy to cook and extremely good. Pork Tikka can be served as a main course with a yogurt dish to temper the spices, or as a starter with a crisp salad.

SERVES 3–4
as a main course
and 6–8
as an entrée

Preparation and
cooking time: 22
minutes (plus
marinating time)

Marinade
1 onion
4 cloves of garlic
5cm (2 inch) piece of ginger
2 green chillies
1 tsp ground cumin
1 tsp ground coriander
150ml (5 fl oz) plain yogurt
1 tbsp olive oil

450g (1 lb) pork fillet
4 tbsp olive oil
1/2 tsp turmeric
425ml (15 fl oz) curry sauce (page 32)
1 tsp paprika
1 tsp salt
3 tsp garam masala
1 tbsp chopped coriander

■ Process or finely chop the onion, garlic, ginger and chillies and combine with the remaining marinade ingredients.

■ Trim the pork fillet and slice into 2.5cm (1 inch) chunks. Place in a bowl with the marinade, cover and refrigerate for about 2 hours or overnight. Remove from the fridge about 30 minutes before using.

- Heat half the oil in a deep, heavy-based frying pan, add the turmeric, stir once and add the curry sauce. Bring to the boil and cook for about 5 minutes until thick.

- Turn down the heat, stir in the paprika and salt, and simmer gently while cooking the pork.

- Heat the remaining oil in a karahi or large frying pan, and add the meat and marinade. Stir-fry on high for 3–4 minutes until the liquid has evaporated and the meat is starting to brown.

- Add the meat mixture to the sauce, scraping out all the crusty bits that will have stuck to the pan. Stir-fry again on high for 3–4 minutes.

- Turn down the heat and simmer, stirring often, for about 15 minutes or until all the liquid has evaporated and the mixture is rich and dark.

- Stir in the garam masala and stir-fry on low heat for a minute or two. Serve sprinkled with the coriander.

Mangalorean Style Pork Bafath

Mangalore is a coastal state south of Goa. Its cuisine is a product of many influences including those of Goa, Portugal and the Middle East. This dish is based on the Mangalorean style of cooking with the abundant use of roasted spices for aroma and flavour, and the use of tamarind and vinegar for balance and to add a tasty tang. It doesn't have the heat of the Goan vindaloos so the flavour of the spices really shines through.

SERVES 3–4	**Spice mix for roasting**	450g (1 lb) pork fillet
Preparation and cooking time: 35–40 minutes	1 tsp coriander seeds	4 tbsp olive oil
	1/2 tsp cumin seeds	1 tsp tamarind paste dissolved in 1 tbsp warm water
	4 dried red chillies	1 onion, thinly sliced
	6 black peppercorns	1 clove garlic, thinly sliced
	2.5cm (1 inch) stick of cinnamon	425ml (15 fl oz) curry sauce (page 32)
	2 cloves	1 tsp salt
	1/2 tsp turmeric	1 tsp paprika
	2 black cardamom pods (optional)	2 tsp dark balsamic vinegar
		1 green chilli, finely sliced

■ Roast the spices in a small pan over medium heat for about a minute or until aromatic. Remove from the pan and cool. Grind to a fine powder in a pestle and mortar or electric grinder.

■ Trim the pork fillet and slice into large chunks about 3cm (1 1/4 inch) in size. Combine the pork with 1 tablespoonful of the oil, the spice mix, tamarind, onion and garlic.

■ Heat the rest of the oil in a deep, heavy-based frying pan and add the curry sauce, salt and paprika. Bring to the boil and cook on high heat for about 5 minutes until thick and starting to release the oil. Lower the heat and simmer gently while cooking the meat.

■ Heat a karahi or frying pan and stir-fry the meat mixture for about 3 minutes until browned. Add the meat to the thickened sauce, scraping the karahi to remove all the crusty bits, and stir in the vinegar and roast spices.

■ Cover and simmer gently for 10 minutes, stirring once or twice. Remove the lid and simmer for a further 10 minutes until the meat is cooked through. Add a little water if the mixture becomes too dry or sticks to the bottom of the pan during this time.

■ Stir in the green chilli and serve.

PORK AND SPROUTS

A Punjabi innovation, this dish combines the richness of pork with the freshness of sprouts and it is a combination that is incredibly good. Traditionally, the dish would be made with pork shoulder or rib, with lots of bone and fat to 'roast' the spices and add plenty of flavour. This recipe uses pork fillet, making it a healthier option, and is quick and easy to prepare.

It is only worth making this dish around wintertime when fresh, sweet sprouts are in season. At other times of the year try a variation with shredded cabbage or spinach.

SERVES 4	400g (14 oz) pork fillet	250g (9 oz) Brussels sprouts
Preparation and cooking time: 30 minutes	4 tbsp olive oil	2 ripe tomatoes, chopped
	1 tsp turmeric	1 tsp salt
	2 green chillies, finely sliced (or half a portion of prepared chilli, page 30)	425ml (15 fl oz) curry sauce (page 32)
	2 cloves of garlic, finely sliced	1 tsp garam masala
	2.5cm (1 inch) piece of ginger, finely sliced (or a portion of prepared garlic and ginger mix, page 30, thawed)	

■ Trim the pork fillet and slice into 2.5cm (1 inch) pieces. Place in a bowl with 1 tablespoonful of the oil, half the turmeric, the chillies, garlic and ginger. Mix well and set aside.

■ Slice off the exposed end of the stalks and remove outer leaves from the sprouts. Rinse under cold water and cut into quarters. Place in a microwave-proof container with 2 tablespoonfuls of water, and microwave on high for 3 minutes.

■ Heat the remaining oil in a deep, heavy-based frying pan and add the tomatoes, salt and remaining turmeric. Cook, stirring for 2 or 3 minutes until the tomato is pulpy.

■ Stir in the pork and stir-fry on medium to high heat for 3 minutes. Add the curry sauce and sprouts to the pan, and bring to the boil, stirring often. Cover the pan and simmer for 10–12 minutes.

■ Remove the lid and simmer for a further 5 minutes, stirring often, until the liquid has evaporated.

■ Stir in the garam masala, heat through for a minute and serve.

CHILLI PORK

A colourful and tasty dish, Chilli Pork is inspired by Chinese influences and will appeal to those who relish the flavour and aroma of fresh chillies. By using the larger (often called Thai) chillies, the colour and flavour are achieved without the extra heat. Use a combination of hot and mild chillies if you prefer a hotter dish.

SERVES 4	500g (1 lb 2 oz) pork fillet, sliced into strips	1 tsp salt
	2 cloves of garlic, finely sliced	4 large, mild green chillies, de-seeded and sliced into
Preparation and	2.5cm (1 inch) piece of ginger, finely sliced	thin strips
cooking time:	(or a portion of prepared garlic and ginger mix,	4 large, mild red chillies, de-seeded and sliced into
30 minutes	page 30, thawed)	thin strips
	1/2 tsp turmeric	1/2 red capsicum, thinly sliced
	4 tbsp olive oil	1 ripe tomato, sliced into 8
	425ml (15 fl oz) curry sauce (page 32)	1 1/2 tsp garam masala
	1/2 tsp chilli powder or to taste	2 tbsp chopped coriander

- Combine the pork, garlic, ginger, turmeric and 1 tablespoonful of the oil in a bowl.

- Heat 1 tablespoonful of the oil in a deep, heavy-based frying pan and add the pork. Stir-fry the meat for 3 minutes on high. Add the curry sauce, chilli powder and salt, and simmer for 10 minutes.

- Meanwhile, heat the remaining oil in a separate pan and add the sliced chillies and capsicum. Stir-fry on medium heat for 3 minutes until starting to colour.

- Stir the fried chillies and capsicum into the pork mixture and simmer for a further 5 minutes before adding the tomato and garam masala.

- Simmer gently for 5 minutes. The sauce should be very thick with the oil separating from it.

- Serve sprinkled with the coriander.

15. SEAFOOD DISHES

FISH AND seafood preparations are prominent in the coastal states of India, where the Arabian Sea, Bay of Bengal and Indian Ocean yield their rich bounties of fish and shellfish. The entire west coast of India is renowned for its seafood dishes. For people living along the Indian coastline, fried, steamed, curried and even pickled seafood is a firm favourite. Families rise early to reach the fish markets in anticipation of the catch of the day.

Seafood dishes menu

Prawn Baadsha with Poori
King prawns sautéed with spring onions, capsicum and spices, and served in a hot creamy sauce with poori (fried Indian bread).

Fish Masala
Juicy fish fillets, marinated and pan-fried, served with a tangy hot sauce flavoured with a touch of yogurt, tomatoes and fresh herbs.

Fish Ambotik
Marinated fillets of fish cooked in a sweet and sour sauce, flavoured with cloves, tamarind and whole red chillies.

Prawn Malabar
Fresh prawns cooked with sautéed onions, capsicum, tomatoes and coconut, and finished with a touch of cream.

Palak Fish
Chunks of fresh fish, spinach leaves and fresh fenugreek, sautéed with onions, tomatoes, cumin seeds and green chilli.

Salmon Kalia
A Bengali speciality, whole fillets of fish fried and served in a spicy sauce with a touch of yogurt.

Goan Fish Curry
Marinated fish chunks, flavoured with mustard seeds, curry leaves and whole red chillies, served in a thick, coconut sauce.

Prawn Baadsha with Poori

This is a special occasion dish that is beautiful to look at and sensational to eat. A delectable dish that was once served in the royal palaces to the reigning *Baadshas* (kings and princes), it reflects the flamboyance and decadence of a bygone era. It has a lovely combination of flavours in a deliciously creamy sauce.

SERVES 4

Preparation and cooking time: 20 minutes

24 king prawns
2 spring onions, chopped
2 green garlic tops, chopped (optional)
1/2 red capsicum, sliced into strips
1 tsp turmeric
2 green chillies, finely chopped
1/2 tsp fennel seeds
1 tsp ground coriander
3 tbsp olive oil
2.5cm (1 inch) stick of cinnamon

425ml (15 fl oz) curry sauce (page 32)
1 tsp salt
4 tbsp yogurt
4 tbsp thick cream
2 tbsp ground almonds
1/2 tsp chilli powder
1/2 tsp garam masala
1 ripe tomato, sliced into 8 wedges
2 tbsp chopped coriander

■ Shell and de-vein the prawns. Rinse, drain and pat dry with paper towels. Combine with the spring onions, garlic tops if using, capsicum, half the turmeric, chillies, fennel seeds, coriander and 1 tablespoonful of the oil. Set aside.

■ Heat the remaining oil in a deep, heavy-based frying pan and add the cinnamon stick and stir for a few seconds. Add the prawn mixture and stir-fry for about a minute.

■ Stir in the curry sauce and salt, and bring to the boil. Cook on medium heat for about 3 minutes until the sauce thickens slightly. Turn down to a simmer.

■ Stir in the yogurt, cream, almonds and chilli powder. Simmer gently for 5 minutes. Stir through the garam masala, tomatoes and half the coriander. Simmer for a minute.

■ Serve sprinkled with the remaining coriander accompanied by pooris (page 160).

FISH MASALA

This dish is really quick and easy to prepare and has a lovely creamy and colourful sauce. The key to a really good Fish Masala is to buy the freshest fish you can.

SERVES 4		
Preparation and cooking time: 20 minutes	500g (1 lb 2 oz) fish fillets (any firm-fleshed white fish) 1 tsp salt 1 tsp turmeric 1/2 tsp chilli powder 3 tbsp olive oil 2 spring onions, sliced 2 green garlic tops, sliced (optional)	2 tsp tomato paste (tomato purée double concentrate) 425ml (15 fl oz) curry sauce (page 32) 1 green chilli, finely sliced 2 tbsp plain yogurt 4 cherry tomatoes, halved 1/2 tsp garam masala 1 tbsp thick cream 2 tbsp chopped coriander

■ Rinse the fish fillets and pat dry with paper towels. Slice into large chunks.

■ Combine half the salt, half the turmeric, the chilli powder and 1 tablespoonful of the oil with the fish pieces, and set aside.

■ Heat the remaining oil in a deep, heavy-based frying pan and add the spring onions and garlic tops if using. Stir-fry for 3 minutes. Stir in the tomato paste and cook for a minute more.

■ Add the curry sauce with the remaining salt and turmeric, and bring to the boil. Cook the sauce on high for about 5 minutes until thickened.

■ Stir the chilli and yogurt into the sauce and cook, stirring until completely incorporated. Lower the heat and simmer gently while cooking the fish.

■ Heat a separate frying pan or karahi and stir-fry the fish on high heat for a minute or two until lightly browned. Add the fish to the sauce and simmer for 5 minutes.

■ Stir in the tomatoes, garam masala, cream and half the coriander. Simmer for a minute and serve sprinkled with the remaining coriander.

FISH AMBOTIK

This is another south Indian delicacy thought to have originated in Goa and undergone modification over time by the Mangaloreans and other southern states. The delicious sauce has the robust flavours of garlic and mustards seeds, and the sour tamarind is balanced by the addition of sugar and a generous amount of chilli.

SERVES 4

Preparation and cooking time: 20–25 minutes

500g (1 lb 2 oz) firm white fish fillets
2 tsp tamarind paste dissolved in 100ml (3 fl oz) warm water
2 tsp soft brown sugar
1 tsp chilli powder
3 tbsp olive oil
1/2 tsp black mustard seeds

4 cloves garlic, finely chopped
1 tsp ground cumin
1/2 tsp salt
1/2 tsp turmeric
1 ripe tomato, chopped
425ml (15 fl oz) curry sauce (page 32)
4 whole red chillies

■ Rinse the fish, pat dry with paper towels and cut into chunks. Combine the fish, tamarind, sugar and chilli powder in a bowl, and set aside.

■ Heat the oil in a deep, heavy-based frying pan and add the mustard seeds. Stir for a few seconds and add the garlic. Stir-fry for a minute or two and add the cumin, salt and turmeric.

■ Stir in the tomato, cook for a minute and stir in the curry sauce. Bring to the boil and simmer for 5 minutes until thickened slightly.

■ Add the fish and marinade, bring back to the boil and simmer the fish in the sauce for about 5 minutes, stirring carefully, until the fish is cooked through. The sauce should be quite thin.

■ Serve topped with the whole red chillies.

PRAWN MALABAR

Although Malabar is a region in the southern state of India, where food is generally more fiery and pungent, Malabar cuisine is noted for its mild flavours and gentle cooking styles such as steaming or baking. The subtle spicing in this dish is ideally suited to the delicate flavour of fresh prawns. If using frozen prawns, thaw in the fridge overnight and pat dry before using.

SERVES 4

Preparation and cooking time: 20–25 minutes

Spice mix
1 tbsp coriander seeds
1 tbsp poppy seeds
1 tbsp grated coconut (or desiccated coconut)
2.5cm (1 inch) stick of cinnamon
2 cloves
4 green cardamom pods

500g (1 lb 2 oz) de-shelled fresh or frozen prawns
3 tbsp olive oil
2 tbsp sliced onion
$1/2$ red capsicum, sliced
$1/2$ tsp turmeric
425ml (15 fl oz) curry sauce (page 32)
1 tsp salt
6 cherry tomatoes, halved
1 green chilli, finely sliced
1 tbsp thick cream
1 tbsp chopped coriander

■ Grind the spices and coconut to a fine powder in a pestle and mortar or electric grinder. Combine with the prawns and 1 tablespoonful of oil. Set aside.

■ Heat the remaining oil in a deep, heavy-based frying pan and add the onion and capsicum. Stir-fry for 3 minutes until soft and add the turmeric, curry sauce and salt.

■ Bring to the boil and cook on high for 5 minutes until thickened. Turn down the heat and let the sauce simmer very gently.

■ Meanwhile, heat a separate pan or karahi and stir-fry the prawns on medium heat for about 2 minutes. Add to the sauce and simmer for 2 minutes. Stir in the tomatoes and simmer for a further 3 or 4 minutes.

■ Finally, stir in the green chilli and cream. Cook gently for a further 2 minutes and serve, sprinkled with the coriander.

PALAK FISH

This is a tasty dish originating in the north of India where fresh fenugreek (*methi*) is used in abundance. The distinct 'curryish' flavour of the fenugreek beautifully enhances the relatively mild flavour of the fish and spinach in this dish.

SERVES 4	500g (1 lb 2 oz) firm-fleshed white fish	125g (4 oz) spinach leaves, shredded
Preparation and cooking time: 20–25 minutes	3 tbsp olive oil 1 tsp cumin seeds 1 onion, sliced 2 cloves of garlic, finely sliced 2 ripe tomatoes, sliced	125g (4 oz) fresh fenugreek (methi) leaves, shredded 200ml (7 fl oz) curry sauce (page 32) 1 tsp salt 2 green chillies, finely sliced

■ Rinse the fish fillets, pat dry with paper towels and cut into large chunks.

■ Heat the oil in a deep, heavy-based frying pan and add the cumin seeds. Stir-fry for a few seconds and add the onion and garlic. Fry on high heat for 2–3 minutes until soft.

■ Add half the tomatoes and stir around in the hot oil for about a minute before adding the spinach and fenugreek.

■ Stir-fry on high heat for about 3 minutes. Turn down the heat and cook for another 5 minutes, stirring now and again, until the mixture is quite dry.

■ Add the curry sauce and salt and bring to the boil. Simmer for 5 minutes.

■ Stir in the fish and chillies and simmer, uncovered, for a further 10–12 minutes, stirring carefully, until the fish is cooked through and the liquid has almost evaporated.

■ Stir through the remaining tomatoes and serve.

Salmon Kalia

This is a wonderful Bengali delicacy traditionally made with a carp-like fish called *Katla*. The delicious aromatically spiced sauce is flavoured with a special spice blend called *Panch Phoran* (five spices), which complements the oily fish beautifully. Salmon is an excellent substitute for the traditional fish but other varieties of fish can be used instead.

SERVES 4

Preparation and cooking time: 20–25 minutes

Spice blend
1/2 tsp fenugreek seeds
1 tsp black mustard seeds
1 tsp onion seeds
1 tsp fennel seeds
2 tsp cumin seeds

1 tsp turmeric
1 1/2 tsp salt
4 salmon cutlets or fillets about 200g (7 oz) each
2 tbsp olive oil

1 clove of garlic, finely sliced
2 tsp tomato paste (tomato purée double concentrate)
600ml (20 fl oz) curry sauce (page 32)
1 tsp paprika
3 tbsp plain yogurt
1 ripe tomato sliced into 8 wedges (or 4 cherry tomatoes halved)
2 hot red chillies, de-seeded and sliced
1/2 tsp garam masala
2 tbsp chopped coriander

■ Combine all the spices for the spice blend and set aside. Mix half of the turmeric with half of the salt and rub over the fish. Set aside.

- Heat the oil in a deep, heavy-based frying pan and add the spice blend. Stir around in the hot oil for about 20 seconds until the seeds start to pop, and add the garlic. Fry for another few seconds and stir in the tomato paste and remaining turmeric.

- Stir-fry for a minute and add the curry sauce, paprika and the remaining salt. Bring to the boil and cook on high for 2 minutes until thickened slightly. Turn down the heat and stir in the yogurt. Simmer while preparing the fish.

- Heat a separate pan capable of holding all the fish in a single layer. Cook on high heat for a minute each side or until lightly browned.

- Transfer the fish to the sauce and turn the pieces in the sauce until each piece is completely coated.

- Bring to the boil and turn down the heat. Cover and simmer for 10–15 minutes, turning once. Stir in the tomato half way through.

- Transfer to a serving platter or plates, sprinkle with the red chillies, garam masala and coriander. Serve.

Note: This dish needs the extra sauce to counterbalance the richness of the fish.

GOAN FISH CURRY

A traditional fish curry from Goa, which, like most Goan food, is colourful, hot and delicious. This is a quick and easy recipe that doesn't require any curry sauce – the spice mix and coconut milk combine to make a delicious thick sauce. Reduce the number of chillies if you don't want it too hot.

Use any fish of your choice. Tuna and salmon work well with this dish as does any firm-fleshed white fish.

SERVES 4

Preparation and cooking time: 20–25 minutes

Bengali Panch Phoran – Bengali five-spice mix
8 dried red chillies
2 tsp cumin seeds
3 tsp coriander seeds
1 tsp black mustard seeds
1 tsp fenugreek seeds

500g (1 lb 2 oz) fish, cut into large chunks
2 tsp tamarind dissolved in 2 tbsp warm water
1 tsp salt
1 tsp turmeric
2 tbsp olive oil

1 onion, sliced
4 curry leaves
2 cloves garlic, ground to a paste
2.5cm (1 inch) piece of ginger
    (or a portion of prepared garlic and ginger mix, page 30, thawed)
1 ripe tomato, chopped
1/2 tsp paprika
300ml (10 fl oz) coconut milk
100ml (3 fl oz) coconut cream
4 red chillies, slit and de-seeded
1/2 tsp garam masala

- Combine the spices for the spice mix and grind to a fine powder in a pestle and mortar or electric grinder. Set aside.

- Combine the fish with the tamarind, half the salt and half the turmeric, and set aside.

- Heat the oil in a deep, heavy-based frying pan and add the sliced onion. Stir-fry for 4–5 minutes until lightly browned and stir in the curry leaves, spice mix, remaining salt and turmeric. Fry for a few seconds.

- Add the garlic and ginger. Stir-fry for a minute until aromatic and add the tomato. Cook the tomato for a couple of minutes until pulpy and stir in the paprika, coconut milk and cream.

- Bring to the boil and simmer for about 5 minutes until thickened slightly. Stir in the red chillies, fish and marinade, bring back to a simmer and cook for 10 minutes, stirring once or twice until the fish is cooked through.

- Serve sprinkled with garam masala.

16. VEGETABLE AND DHAL DISHES

IT IS VIRTUALLY impossible for a Westerner to imagine sitting down to a good meal without a generous portion of meat, chicken or fish. Yet 70 per cent of the population of the Indian sub-continent is vegetarian and do just that.

Historically, Indian cuisine has been shaped by many influences, the most significant of which is probably vegetarianism, largely brought about by strong religious beliefs beginning with Buddhism and Janism, which came to India around 600 BC. Although these are no longer major religions in India they had the effect of pervading Indian culture and converting its people to a way of life where consuming flesh is strictly against their *dharam* (faith).

There is some scientific evidence to suggest that non-meat eating populations have a lower life expectancy, although there is little to support this in areas where food is fresh and plentiful and poverty and famine do not play a role. Indian vegetarian food is so varied and diverse that it is easy to get sufficient nutrients, protein and fibre without high levels of fat, a balance often lacking in modern Western diets. Fresh, home-made yogurt or curd is eaten at every meal, providing good quality protein and plenty of vitamins and minerals. Pulses, lentils or chickpeas feature daily and, eaten with bread or rice, provide complete proteins and lots of fibre. The addition of fresh or sun-dried herbs and spices gives further nutritional value to the dishes. Even snacks and desserts, often made with besan (chickpea flour) and/or milk, are nutritious. Indian vegetarian food is also delicious due to the myriad of spices, pickles, chutneys and relishes that are consumed at each meal. With this wonderful cuisine it is possible to eat vegetarian dishes every day and not miss eating meat. Indeed, India is quite a paradise for vegetarian food.

Even if you are not vegetarian, the following dishes are good accompaniments that add variety and interest to the meat dishes in the preceding chapters.

VEGETABLE AND DHAL DISHES MENU

CAULIFLOWER KEEMA
Minced cauliflower, cooked with fennel seeds, garlic, ginger and peas. A deliciously 'meaty' dish.

ALOO SOY 'BARI'
Potato and meaty soy chunks in a deliciously spicy gravy flavoured with fresh herbs.

BENGAN KA BHARTA
Roasted, skinless aubergine flesh, finely chopped into a coarse purée and sautéed with onions, tomatoes, spices and herbs.

PALAK PANIR KASOORI
Indian cheese cubes, pan-fried until crisp and tossed with spinach, sun-dried fenugreek leaves, onions, ginger and cumin.

SHABNAM CURRY
Mushrooms, potatoes, peas and cashew nuts cooked in an authentic combination of garlic, ginger and onion flavoured with fresh coriander.

HATHO BRINJAL
A spicy combination of aubergine, potatoes and peas, cooked with fresh tomatoes and shredded coconut.

TARKA DHAL
A quick cook version of this popular dhal, lightly spiced and generously flavoured with fresh herbs.

CAULIFLOWER KEEMA

This is a quick and simple recipe, good as a main dish or side dish with a dhal or meat curry. As with most recipes, fresh cauliflower when it's in season will produce the best results. If you can get it, try it with organic cauliflower, it is even better.

SERVES 4–6

Preparation and cooking time: 30 minutes

1 small cauliflower
3 tbsp olive oil
1/2 tsp fennel seeds
1 ripe tomato, chopped
1 tsp salt
1/2 tsp turmeric

1 green chilli, finely sliced
350ml (13 fl oz) curry sauce (page 32)
150g (5 oz) frozen peas
1/2 tsp garam masala
1 tbsp chopped coriander

■ Break the cauliflower into florets. Rinse and drain well. Place into the bowl of a food processor and process on slow speed until coarsely 'minced'. Or grate or chop finely.

■ Heat the oil in a heavy-based pan and add the fennel seeds, tomato, salt and turmeric. Cook on medium heat for about 2 minutes and stir in the green chilli.

■ Cook for about a minute before adding the cauliflower. Stir for 3–4 minutes on medium heat and add the curry sauce.

■ Bring to the boil and simmer for 15 minutes, stirring occasionally, until the liquid has almost evaporated and the cauliflower is tender.

■ Stir in the peas and garam masala, and cook for a further 5 minutes, stirring often.

■ Serve sprinkled with the coriander.

ALOO SOY 'BARI'

This has become a popular dish amongst Indian vegetarian populations in recent years. The soy chunks are highly nutritious and an excellent substitute for meat, but because they readily absorb the flavours of the sauce they become very tasty too. They are quite unlike the traditional *bari* which can be described as a spicy, sun-dried 'cake' of fermented, ground mung dahl, but they are a convenient and delicious alternative.

Soy nuggets are available from Indian grocers, health food stores and some supermarkets.

SERVES 4	300g (11 oz) soy nuggets	1/2 tsp turmeric
Preparation and cooking time: 30 minutes	2 medium potatoes	425ml (15 fl oz) curry sauce (page 32)
	3 tbsp olive oil	1 tsp salt
	2 spring onions, chopped	400ml (14 fl oz) hot water
	1 tbsp chopped fenugreek (methi) leaves (optional)	1 tsp garam masala
	2 green chillies, finely chopped	2 tbsp chopped coriander
	1/2 tsp cumin seeds	

■ Soak the soy nuggets in enough hot water to cover. Set aside.

■ Peel the potatoes and slice each one into 6 or 8 evenly sized chunks. Boil in salted water for about 10 minutes until just tender but not breaking apart. Drain.

■ Meanwhile, heat the oil in a deep, heavy-based frying pan and fry the spring onion and fenugreek leaves if using, for about 2 minutes.

■ Add the chillies, cumin seeds and turmeric, fry for 30 seconds and stir in the curry sauce and salt. Bring to the boil and cook on medium to high heat for about 5 minutes, stirring frequently until the sauce is thick.

■ Add the drained soy nuggets and about 400ml (14 fl oz) of hot water. Bring to the boil and simmer partly covered for 10 minutes.

■ Add the potatoes and garam masala, and simmer for a further 5 minutes. Stir in the chopped coriander and serve.

Bengan Ka Bharta

Native to India, the aubergine (called *bengan* or *brinjal* in India) is used widely in Indian cuisine. Its incredible versatility allows it to be used in a huge variety of different ways from pickles to curries. Bengan Ka Bharta is another delicious example of the versatility of this King of Vegetables. Traditionally, the aubergines would be roasted in the dying embers of the cooking fire, but microwaving is a quick option.

For this dish, choose large aubergines with a smooth, shiny skin and bright green stalks.

SERVES 4–6

Preparation and cooking time: 40 minutes

2 large aubergines, about 800g (1 lb 12 oz) total weight
4 tbsp olive oil
1 onion, finely chopped
1 tsp cumin seeds
2 cloves of garlic, finely chopped
2.5cm (1 inch) piece of ginger, finely chopped (or a portion of prepared garlic and ginger mix, page 30, thawed)

2 green chillies, finely chopped (or a portion of prepared chilli, page 30)
2 ripe tomatoes, chopped
1 1/2 tsp salt
1/2 tsp turmeric
1 tsp garam masala
2 tbsp chopped coriander

■ Make 3 or 4 large slits along the length of the aubergines and microwave on high for 3 minutes. Turn the aubergines over and microwave again for 2 or 3 minutes or until the vegetables are quite soft. Remember they will continue cooking once the microwave is off. Or roast in a hot oven (220°C, 425°F or gas mark 7) for about 35 minutes. Allow to stand until cool enough to handle.

■ Meanwhile, heat the oil in a deep, heavy-based frying pan and fry the onion and cumin for 3 or 4 minutes until the onion softens.

■ Add the garlic, ginger and chillies, and stir-fry for a minute. Add the tomatoes, salt and turmeric, and cook over low heat for about 10 minutes until the tomatoes are pulpy and the oil starts to separate from the mixture.

■ Meanwhile, peel the aubergines and slice the pulp finely. Add to the pan and mix well over low heat for 3 or 4 minutes.

■ Stir in the garam masala, cook for a minute and add in half the coriander. Serve sprinkled with the remaining coriander.

Palak Panir Kasoori

This is a wonderfully satisfying, substantial and tasty north Indian vegetarian dish. The panir (Indian cheese) combines beautifully with the robust flavours of fenugreek (*methi*).

SERVES 4–6

Preparation and cooking time: 30 minutes

3 tbsp olive oil
1 onion, sliced
1 tsp ground cumin
2.5cm (1 inch) piece of ginger, grated
1 green chilli, finely sliced
250g (9 oz) shredded spinach

200g fresh fenugreek (methi) leaves or 50g (2 oz) dried methi leaves, rinsed
200ml (7 fl oz) curry sauce (page 32)
1 tsp salt
1 quantity of panir (page 24)

- Heat 2 tablespoonfuls of the oil in a deep, heavy-based frying pan, and fry the onion until starting to colour. Stir in the cumin, ginger and green chilli. Fry for a minute until aromatic.

- Add the spinach and fenugreek, and stir-fry on medium heat for 3 minutes. Add the curry sauce and salt, and bring to the boil. Turn down the heat and simmer for 15 minutes, stirring occasionally until all the liquid has evaporated.

- Meanwhile, heat the remainder of the oil in a separate frying pan and fry the panir until golden brown on all sides.

- Add the panir to the vegetables and cook for a further 5 minutes, stirring often.

- Serve.

SHABNAM CURRY

This is another northern Indian dish contributed to Indian cuisine by the Moghuls. It has a thick, dryish sauce and a mild but delicious flavour.

SERVES 4–6 Preparation and cooking time: 30 minutes	1 large or 2 small potatoes 3 tbsp olive oil 2 ripe tomatoes, chopped 1 tsp salt 1 tsp ground coriander 1/2 tsp turmeric 250g (9 oz) button mushrooms, halved	125g (4 oz) fresh or frozen peas 300ml (11 fl oz) curry sauce (page 32) 1/2 tsp chilli powder 2 tbsp cashew nuts, ground to a paste 1/2 tsp garam masala 1 tbsp chopped coriander

■ Peel the potato and cut into 2.5cm (1 inch) chunks. Cook in boiling salted water until just tender. Drain.

■ Meanwhile, heat the oil in a deep, heavy-based frying pan and add the tomatoes and salt. Stir-fry for 4–5 minutes until the tomatoes are pulpy and the oil separates.

■ Stir in the coriander and turmeric and fry for a minute. Add the mushrooms and peas and stir-fry on medium heat for 5 minutes.

■ Add the curry sauce, chilli powder and potato and bring to the boil. Turn down the heat and simmer gently for 5 minutes, stirring now and again.

■ Stir in the cashew nut paste and garam masala, and simmer for a further 5 minutes, stirring often.

■ Serve sprinkled with the coriander.

Hatho Brinjal

Aubergine, or eggplant as it is known in some parts of the world, is a common and popular vegetable in Indian cooking. Easy to grow and nutritious, it is incredibly versatile. It can be fried, roasted, stuffed, mashed, pickled and anything in between!

Good on its own, it also marries well with potatoes as in this south Indian dish.

SERVES 4–6

Preparation and cooking time: 30 minutes

4 small aubergines (approx. 250g or 9 oz)
1 large or 2 small potatoes
4 tbsp olive oil
1 tsp ground cumin
1 tsp ground coriander
2 ripe tomatoes, chopped
1 tsp salt

1 tsp turmeric
2 tbsp grated coconut (or desiccated coconut)
350ml (13 fl oz) curry sauce (page 32)
1 tsp chilli powder
100g (3 oz) frozen peas
1/2 tsp garam masala
1 tbsp chopped coriander

■ Slice each aubergine in half and each half into 3 or 4 thick slices depending on the size of the aubergine. Peel the potatoes and cut into slices a little smaller than the aubergine.

■ Heat the oil in a deep, heavy-based frying pan, add the cumin and coriander and fry for a few seconds.

- Stir in the tomatoes and salt and cook for 2–3 minutes, and add the turmeric and coconut. Stir-fry for a minute and add the potato and aubergine.
- Stir-fry for about 3 minutes on medium heat and add the curry sauce and chilli powder. Bring to the boil, cover and simmer for 15 minutes, stirring once or twice until the vegetables are tender. Add a little water if the sauce is becoming too dry.

- Add the peas and simmer, uncovered, for a further 5 minutes until the liquid has evaporated.

- Stir in the garam masala and simmer for a minute. Serve sprinkled with coriander.

TARKA DHAL

This easy cook, one-pot recipe is a godsend when you need something quick and simple as a side dish. It goes well with any meat or vegetable curry and is also great with tandoori meats to make a complete meal.

Leaving the salt until the end helps the lentils cook a lot quicker.

SERVES 4	4 heaped tbsp good quality red split lentils	1 ripe tomato, chopped
Preparation and cooking time: 35–40 minutes	425ml (15 fl oz) water 1 small onion, chopped 3 cloves of garlic, finely chopped 2 tbsp olive oil 1/4 tsp turmeric	1 green chilli, finely chopped 1 level tsp salt 1/2 tsp garam masala 1 tbsp finely chopped coriander

- Rinse the lentils in two or three changes of water and place in a pan with all the other ingredients except the salt, garam masala and coriander.

- Bring to the boil and simmer, uncovered, for about 10 minutes, stirring now and again. Cover the pan and simmer for a further 20 minutes, stirring two or three times. Add a little more water if the dhal looks too thick.

- Stir in the salt, garam masala and half the coriander. Serve sprinkled with the remaining coriander.

17. BIRYANIS

BIRYANI is to India what risotto is to Italy and the paella is to Spain, only more so. There is amongst Indians an intense patriotism about this sumptuous dish; a sense of pride and splendour. In many parts of India, no lavish feast could lay claim to that status without the presence of biryani.

The true biryani is indeed a magnificent dish; the best basmati rice layered with succulent meats in delicious sauces, flavoured with exquisite 'sweet' spices such as saffron, cardamom, cinnamon, cloves and nutmeg, gently baked in sealed pots until the aromas and flavours permeate the layers and, finally, adorned with expensive ingredients like almonds, pistachios, cashews and dried fruits braised in pure ghee (clarified butter).

Its attraction is legendary. One legend has it that biryani was created by the beautiful Mumtaz Mahal, the queen of King Shah Jehan (the famous Taj Mahal was built by the king as her tomb after she died during childbirth), as a means of providing a complete meal to feed their army.

With such a lavish concoction, the princely Moghuls inevitably played a significant part in the creation of the biryani. Food historians believe that the dish originated in Persia and was introduced to India by the extravagant, food-loving Moghuls during the early part of the sixteenth century. Indeed, the word 'biryani' is derived from the Persian word 'birian', which means 'fried or roasted before cooking'.

The popularity and importance of biryani quickly spread throughout the Middle East, South Asia and Southeast Asia, and an enormous variety of biryanis have been developed, many taking on the name of the region or the ruler of the time. So high was the status granted to this dish, there are claims that the earlier Punjabi 'Nawabs' (provincial governors or viceroys of regions during the Moghul era) wore a particular turban for each variety of biryani popular in the region.

Traditionally, goat meat was used to make biryani, but nowadays it is usual to use lamb, chicken, fish and vegetables of all types. The common threads are the layers of cooked rice between the meat and vegetables, the 'dum' (sealed pot) style of cooking, and the unfading importance still attached to this fabulous dish.

PREPARATION FOR BIRYANIS
A good biryani should be spicy with lots of sweet and savoury aromas, but never hot. Traditional biryanis, like many other traditional Indian dishes, incorporate a dozen or more

spices and take hours of preparation and cooking, with each variety of biryani differing in the combination of spices used according to the style of cooking of the region.

Restaurant methods simplify the process by the prior preparation of meat, sauces and basic spice blends, adding specific ingredients as required for a particular recipe. You can use chicken as prepared for chicken curries (page 59) or lamb as prepared for lamb curries (page 71).

You will also need to prepare a small quantity of the following biryani spice mix:

Biryani spice blend

1 tsp green cardamom pods
1 tsp cloves
1 tsp fennel seeds
1 tsp mace
2 tsp cumin seeds
2 x 2.5cm (1 inch) sticks of cinnamon
1 nutmeg, crushed

Grind all the ingredients to a fine powder in an electric grinder or pestle and mortar. Place in a small jar, label and store in a cool, dark place for no more than 6 weeks for best results.

Accompaniments to Biryani

A good biryani is full of flavour and aroma but it is quite a 'dry' dish. Traditionally it is served with yogurt preparations, pickles, spicy salads and chutneys, and does not require a sauce or gravy. However, restaurant biryanis generally come with a curry sauce on the side to satisfy the Western penchant for gravy. I have included recipes for traditional and modern accompaniments to the biryani.

Ulli Surka (onion and chilli salad)

1 red onion, sliced
2 green chillies, de-seeded and sliced
3 tbsp water
1/2 tsp salt flakes

Combine all the ingredients in a small bowl, crushing the chillies with the back of a spoon to release the flavours. Allow to stand for about 30 minutes before serving.

Biryani Chammanthi

6 tbsp grated fresh coconut
2 green chillies, coarsely chopped
2 tsp grated ginger
Handful of mint leaves
Handful of coriander
120ml (4 fl oz) yogurt
1/2 tsp salt

Grind the coconut, chillies, ginger, mint and coriander to a coarse paste. Combine with the yogurt and salt.

Yogurt Chutney

250ml (9 fl oz) plain yogurt
6 tbsp shredded coriander leaves
3 tbsp shredded mint leaves
2 green chillies, finely sliced
1 clove of garlic, finely sliced
1/2 tsp ambchoor
1/2 tsp salt

Combine all the ingredients in a small bowl. Allow to stand for 30 minutes before serving.

Curry Sauce

500ml (18 fl oz/1 US pint) curry sauce (page 32)
1 tsp chilli powder
1/2 tsp paprika
1/2 tsp salt
1/2 tsp garam masala

In a clean pan, bring the curry sauce to the boil and simmer for 5 minutes until thickened slightly. Stir in the remaining ingredients. Simmer for a minute and serve.

Biryani menu

Malabar Prawn Biryani
Gentle spice aromas with succulent prawns.

Calicut Chicken Biryani
Chicken pieces with fresh herbs and aromatic spices.

Shahi Biryani
A sumptuous lamb dish cooked in the lavish style of the grand Moghul emperors.

Hyderabadi Vegetable Biryani
A vegetarian dish that combines the rich creamy style of north Indian cuisine and the pungent, sharp flavours of the south.

MALABAR PRAWN BIRYANI

Malabar is a region of southern India nestling along the southwest coast of the Indian peninsula. Its cuisine is generally milder and gentler than that of its immediate neighbours. The Malabar region is synonymous with biryani, and seafood, such as the prawns in this recipe, is a common ingredient in many of its dishes.

SERVES 4	4 tbsp olive oil	100ml (3 fl oz) coconut milk
	1 onion, sliced	2 tsp lemon juice
Preparation and cooking time: 35 minutes	4 bay leaves, fresh or dried	1 tsp salt
	1 tsp biryani spice blend (page 144)	800g (1 lb 12 oz) saffron pilau rice (page 166)
	1 green chilli, finely sliced	1 tbsp grated coconut
	450g (1 lb) raw prawns	1 tbsp chopped coriander
	300ml (11 fl oz) curry sauce (page 32)	

■ Pre-heat the oven to 200°C, 400°F or gas mark 6.

■ Heat the oil in a deep, heavy-based frying pan and add the onion. Fry on medium heat for about 3 minutes until translucent.

■ Add the bay leaves, spice blend and chilli, and fry for another minute. Stir in the prawns and stir-fry for 2 minutes.

■ Add the curry sauce, coconut milk, lemon juice and salt. Bring to the boil and simmer for 5 minutes.

■ Meanwhile, microwave the rice on high for 2 minutes. Fluff up the rice gently with a fork and place half in a deep ovenproof dish with a tight-fitting lid.

■ Spoon the prawn mixture over the rice layer and cover with the remaining rice. Put the lid firmly on the dish and place in the oven for 20 minutes.

■ Serve sprinkled with the grated coconut and coriander, and with accompaniments of choice.

CALICUT CHICKEN BIRYANI

Calicut is a city in the southern Indian coastal state of Kerala. Its cuisine has been described as one of the world's earliest fusion cuisines with influences from the Tamils, Arabs, East Asians, Sinhalese and even the Moghuls.

Calicut is famous for its biryanis, typically served with vinegary pickles and popadoms.

SERVES 4

Preparation and cooking time: 35 minutes

3 tbsp olive oil
6 curry leaves, fresh or frozen
2 cloves of garlic, finely chopped
2.5cm (1 inch) piece of ginger, finely chopped
    (or a portion of prepared garlic and ginger mix, page 30, thawed)
2 green chillies, finely chopped (or half a portion of prepared chillies, page 30)
1/2 tsp turmeric
1 tsp biryani spice blend (page 144)
1 tsp poppy seeds, ground to a paste
425ml (15 fl oz) curry sauce (page 32)

1/2 tsp salt
450g (1 lb) cooked chicken (page 59)
200ml (7 fl oz) plain yogurt
2 tbsp chopped coriander
2 tbsp chopped mint leaves
1 tbsp lime juice
800g (1 lb 12 oz) pilau rice (page 163)
2 tbsp melted ghee (clarified butter, page 24)
1 tbsp raw cashew nuts
1 tbsp sultanas
1 hard boiled egg, sliced

■ Pre-heat the oven to 200°C, 400°F or gas mark 6.

■ Heat the oil in a deep, heavy-based frying pan and add the curry leaves, garlic, ginger and chillies. Fry for a minute or two on medium heat and add the turmeric, biryani spice blend and poppy seed paste. Cook for another minute.

■ Stir in the curry sauce and salt and bring to the boil. Boil for 5 minutes and add the chicken and yogurt.

■ Bring back to the boil and simmer for 3 minutes. Turn off the heat and stir in the coriander, mint and lime juice.

■ Meanwhile, microwave the rice on high for 2 minutes. Fluff up the rice gently with a fork and place half in a deep ovenproof dish with a tight-fitting lid.

■ Spoon the chicken mixture over the rice layer and cover with the remaining rice. Put the lid firmly on the dish and place in the oven for 20 minutes.

■ Heat the ghee in a small pan and gently braise the cashew nuts and sultanas until the nuts turn a pale golden brown and the sultanas plump up.

■ Serve the biryani garnished with the egg slices and sprinkled with the nuts and sultanas.

SHAHI BIRYANI

Moghlai cuisine, so named because it originates from the era of the grand Moghuls, is renowned for being rich and lavish. Among the many and varied cuisines that were to become native to India, this one has been at the forefront of shaping the way Indians cook and eat today. This delicious dish is testament to that magnificent era.

SERVES 4

Preparation and cooking time: 45 minutes

4 tbsp melted ghee (clarified butter, page 24)
2 tbsp almonds, blanched
2 tbsp golden raisins
1 tsp saffron
4 tbsp milk, warmed
3 tbsp olive oil
1 onion, sliced
2 cloves of garlic, finely sliced
1 1/2 tsp biryani spice blend (page 144)

425ml (15 fl oz) curry sauce (page 32)
1/2 tsp chilli powder
1/2 tsp salt
450g (1 lb) cooked lamb (page 71)
100ml (3 fl oz) plain yogurt
100ml (3 fl oz) single cream
1/2 tsp garam masala
1 tbsp chopped coriander
800g (1 lb 12 oz) saffron pilau rice (page 166)

■ Pre-heat the oven to 200°C, 400°F or gas mark 6.

■ Heat the ghee in a small pan and gently braise the almonds and raisins until the nuts have turned a pale golden brown, and the raisins have plumped up. Set aside.

■ Add the saffron to the warmed milk, stir and set aside.

■ Heat the oil in a deep, heavy-based frying pan and add the onion. Stir-fry on medium heat until crisp. Remove with a slotted spoon and set aside.

■ Add the garlic to the oil remaining in the pan and stir-fry for a few seconds. Stir in the spice blend and cook for a further few seconds until aromatic.

■ Add the curry sauce, chilli powder and salt, and bring to the boil. Cook on high heat for 5 minutes until the sauce is thick.

■ Stir in the lamb and yogurt, and bring back to the boil. Simmer for 5 minutes and stir in the cream. Bring back to a gentle simmer and simmer for a further 5 minutes before stirring in the garam masala and coriander.

■ Meanwhile, microwave the rice on high for 2 minutes. Fluff up the rice gently with a fork and place half in a deep ovenproof dish with a tight-fitting lid. Sprinkle over half the onion, almonds, raisins, melted ghee and saffron milk.

■ Spoon the lamb mixture over the rice layer and cover with the remaining rice. Sprinkle over the remaining onion, almonds, raisins, melted ghee and saffron milk.

■ Put the lid firmly on the dish and place in the oven for 20 minutes. Serve with accompaniments of choice.

Breads menu

Plain Nan
Leavened flat bread, deliciously light, puffy and soft, brushed with extra virgin olive oil.

Garlic Nan
Leavened flat bread, sprinkled with finely chopped fresh garlic.

Peshwari Nan
Leavened flat bread, stuffed with toasted nuts and dried fruit.

Mirchi Nan
Leavened flat bread, sprinkled with marinated onions and sliced green chillies.

Stuffed Paratha
Unleavened wholewheat flat bread, layered with butter, stuffed with spicy potatoes and pan-fried with virgin olive oil until crispy.

Poori
Unleavened wholewheat flat bread, deep-fried until puffed and golden.

BASIC NAN RECIPE

This is a really simple recipe but it produces wonderful results. If you have a bread-maker, use it on the dough setting, but only let it knead for about 5 minutes. Dough that's kneaded long enough to make good bread loaves becomes too elastic to roll out easily. You can leave the dough to rise in the bread pan with the machine switched off.

MAKES 6 NAN	300ml approx. (11 fl oz) water	1 tbsp oil
Preparation time: 10 minutes plus about an hour to prove the dough	2 tsp sugar	450g (1 lb) white bread flour or plain white flour
	3 tsp instant dried yeast	1 tsp salt

- Warm the water slightly, pour into a large bowl and add the sugar, yeast and oil.

- Add the flour and sprinkle the salt over the flour. Using your hand, mix and bring the ingredients together, adding more water or more flour until you have a soft but non-sticky dough.

- Place the dough onto a clean, lightly floured surface and knead it for 5 minutes until smooth.

- Put the dough in a lightly greased bowl, cover with a damp tea towel or greased cling wrap. Stand the bowl in a draught-free place for about an hour or until the dough has doubled in size.

- De-gas the dough by punching it down and knead briefly before using.

- The dough can be kept in the fridge for up to 2 days. It will rise, quite quickly at first until it cools down, so check it frequently and punch it down.

Freezing: The dough can be frozen for up to a month.

TIP

If you are planning to make several nan, have sheets of baking paper or thick kitchen paper handy. Roll out your nan, place on a sheet of paper and place another sheet of paper on top. Repeat with up to 6 nan; any more and you might find the bottom ones stick. Cook as soon as possible.

Plain Nan

MAKES 6 NAN

Preparation and cooking time: 20 minutes

1 quantity of basic nan dough (page 153)
1 tbsp extra virgin olive oil

- Divide the dough into 6 portions.

- Roll a portion into a thin round or tear shape and cook on a hot tava or frying pan for about 2 minutes each side until puffed with brown spots starting to appear.

- Alternatively, cook the underside on the tava and place under a very hot grill for about a minute to cook the top.

- Wrap in a clean tea towel to keep warm while cooking the remaining nan.

- Brush with the oil and serve.

GARLIC NAN

MAKES 6 NAN

Preparation and
cooking time:
20 minutes

1 quantity of basic nan dough (page 153)
1 tbsp extra virgin olive oil
3 cloves of garlic, finely chopped

■ Divide the dough into 6 portions.

■ Roll a portion into a thin round or tear shape, brush with the oil and sprinkle with the garlic. Press the garlic down into the dough very lightly.

■ Cook the nan on a hot tava or frying pan for about 2 minutes and place under a very hot grill for a further minute or so.

■ Wrap in a clean tea towel to keep warm while cooking the remaining nan.

Peshwari Nan

MAKES 6 NAN

Preparation and
cooking time:
30 minutes

2 tbsp almonds, blanched
2 tbsp pistachios
2 tbsp raisins
2 tsp caster sugar

1 quantity of basic nan dough (page 153)
1 tbsp flaked almonds
1 tbsp extra virgin olive oil

■ Roast the nuts in a hot pan on gentle heat until the almonds are starting to colour. Cool.

■ Chop the nuts and raisins finely, or process briefly in a food processor and combine with the sugar. Set aside.

■ Divide the dough into 6 portions. Roll one portion into a thick round and place about 1 tablespoonful of the nut and raisin mixture onto one half of the round, about 2.5cm (1 inch) from the edge.

■ Dampen the edges slightly with water and bring the other half over the mixture and press to seal the edges.

■ Carefully roll out the nan, stretching it to form a tear-drop shape. Sprinkle with flaked almonds, pressing them down into the dough lightly.

■ Cook the nan on a hot tava or frying pan for about 2 minutes and place under a very hot grill for a further minute or so.

■ Wrap in a clean tea towel to keep warm while cooking the remaining nan.

■ Brush with olive oil and serve hot.

MIRCHI NAN

MAKES 6 NAN	1 onion, finely sliced	$1/2$ tsp ground coriander
Preparation and cooking time: 40 minutes	$1/2$ tsp salt 2 green chillies, de-seeded and finely sliced $1/2$ tsp ground cumin	1 quantity of basic nan dough (page 153) 1 tbsp extra virgin olive oil

- Combine the onion and salt in a small bowl and allow to stand for about 20 minutes. Drain off any liquid and mix in the chillies, cumin and coriander.

- Divide the dough into 6 portions.

- Roll a portion into a thin round or tear-drop shape, brush with oil and sprinkle with the onion and chilli mixture, pressing it down into the dough very lightly.

- Cook the nan on a hot tava or frying pan for about 2 minutes and place under a very hot grill for a further minute or so. Brush with more olive oil.

- Wrap in a clean tea towel to keep warm while cooking the remaining nan.

STUFFED PARATHA

These delicious breads are a meal in themselves but they can also be served with dhals and curries for a substantial accompaniment.

MAKES 4 PARATHA	225g (8 oz) chapatti flour, plus extra for dusting	¹/₂ tsp turmeric
Preparation and cooking time: 30 minutes	110ml (4 fl oz) water 1 large potato, grated 1 tsp salt 1 tsp garam masala	2 green chillies, finely chopped or 1 tsp chilli powder 50g (2 oz) butter, softened 4 tbsp extra virgin olive oil

■ Place the flour in a large mixing bowl and slowly add the water, mixing the flour and water together until you have a soft, pliable dough.

■ Using damp hands, knead the dough briefly, fold into a neat shape, cover and set aside for 10–15 minutes.

■ Squeeze excess liquid out of the potato and combine with the salt, garam masala, turmeric and chillies.

■ Heat a tava or heavy-based frying pan on low to medium heat. Take two golf-size pieces of dough and, using the extra flour for dusting, roll both out to about the size of a saucer.

- Spread a little butter on one round of dough to about 2.5cm (1 inch) from the edge and cover with about 1 tablespoonful of the potato filling.

- Place the second round of dough over the potato filling and press to seal the edges. Dust with flour and roll out to about the size of a dinner plate.

- Slap the paratha from one hand to the other to remove any excess flour, which will burn if left on.

- Place onto a medium hot tava and brush or spray olive oil onto the upper side. Flip over and brush or spray the other side with oil.

- Cook for about 30 seconds and flip over and brush with a little more oil. Repeat the process after a further 30 seconds or so.

- If the tava or pan is at the right heat, the paratha should take about 3 minutes to cook. When cooked, the paratha will be crisp at the edges and a nice golden brown with large dark-brown spots. If those spots are black, the heat is too high; if they are not brown enough, the heat is not high enough.

- Wrap the paratha loosely in foil to keep it warm while making the remaining parathas. Serve hot with achar (pickles) and spiced yogurt.

TIP

For a variation, boil and mash the potato instead of grating it. Allow it to cool, mix with the spices and proceed as above.

POORI

These deep-fried little breads are often made with plain white flour, but I think wholewheat chapatti flour gives them a better flavour. Pooris are a good choice if you are planning to serve a large number of people as they are quick to prepare and re-heat well.

MAKES 18–20 POORI	450g (1 lb) chapatti flour, plus extra for dusting
Preparation and cooking time: 30 minutes	1 tsp salt
	220ml (8 fl oz) water
	Oil for deep-frying

■ Place the flour in a large mixing bowl, sprinkle with the salt and slowly add the water, mixing the flour and water together until you have a soft, pliable dough.

■ Using damp hands, knead the dough briefly, fold into a neat shape, cover and set aside for 10–15 minutes.

■ Fill a karahi or deep saucepan about two-thirds full of oil and heat the oil to hot but not smoking.

■ Take a piece of dough about the size of a golf ball and roll into a round about 15cm (6 inches) in diameter and very thin (about 1mm thick). Repeat with 3–5 more pieces of dough depending on the size of your karahi.

■ Quickly slide the pooris into the hot oil. They should rise to the surface within about 6 seconds and begin to puff up. As they do, gently flip them over for a few seconds to lightly brown the other side. The whole process should take about 15 seconds.

■ Remove the pooris and drain them on a wire rack placed over a tray. Repeat with the remaining dough.

■ Serve immediately or wrap in foil. Reheat for a few seconds in the microwave or place on a baking tray, cover with foil and put in a hot oven for about 15 minutes.

19. RICE DISHES

THERE IS SOME speculation about the origins of rice but it appears to have a long history going back to 3000 BC when, it is believed, Indian natives discovered the rice plant growing in the wild and began experimenting with it. Today, rice is grown and harvested on every continent with the exception of Antarctica, where growing conditions are completely unsuitable.

Two-thirds of the world's population relies on rice as a food source. Rice is the staple food of 65 per cent of the Indian population and has become in more recent times the principal crop grown in the country. Rice cultivation is carried out in all Indian states – many would say to the detriment of the environment due to the crop's high water requirement – and India now ranks second only to China in world rice production. Rice-based industries are a source of employment and income for more than 50 million households within India.

Although about 600 new varieties of rice have been developed during the last 30 years, basmati rice remains the most prized. The basmati grain is slender and aromatic with a nutty flavour and superior cooking qualities for a light, fluffy, flavoursome result.

Rice is versatile, nutritious, healthy, non-allergenic and gluten free. It is naturally low in fat, cholesterol and sodium, and has only 200 calories per cup cooked. Products such as alcoholic liquor (Sake), glue and even clothing are made from rice or rice products in the rice-producing regions throughout the world.

It is no wonder, then, that the grain is regarded with such reverence within many cultures, that it is used for religious offerings, and to throw leftover rice away is considered sinful. To add to its virtues, uncooked white rice can be kept indefinitely as long as it is kept dry, and uncooked basmati rice actually improves with age.

To prevent any bacteria in the rice from causing food poisoning, it's best to serve rice when it has just been cooked. However, if that is not possible, you should cool the rice as quickly as possible (ideally within one hour) and keep it in the fridge for no more than one day until reheating. Reheated rice should be piping hot and rice should not be reheated more than once.

PILAU RICE DISHES

Here are a few simple tips to help make rice cooking a breeze:

- Always measure the rice and water carefully to ensure that you get a perfect result with the rice grains firm and separate, and not soft and soggy. One measure of rice to one-and-a-half measures of water are the perfect proportions for savoury basmati rice dishes.

- Drain the rice well after washing it to ensure it is quite dry before cooking (some cooks say rice should never be washed, but I prefer to wash it).

- Always cook the rice well in oil or ghee as directed. This cooks the outer layer of starch and helps keep the grains separate.

- Once the water is boiling, keep the heat as low as possible and ensure the pot is well sealed with a tight fitting lid. 'Dry off' in a warm oven for a few minutes if possible.

- Gently fluff up the rice before serving.

Rice dishes menu

Pilau Rice
Basmati rice, flavoured with whole spices and ghee.

Egg Fried Rice
Basmati rice with fried egg.

Peshwari Pilau
Basmati rice with almonds, pistachios and dried fruit.

Saffron Pilau
Basmati rice, delicately flavoured with saffron and cardamom.

Mushroom Pilau
Basmati rice with mushroom.

PILAU RICE

Colourful and beautifully aromatic, this is still the most popular of the rice dishes on the restaurant menu. Its appearance, however, relies on artificial food colourings. If you don't like the idea of that, leave them out; they don't contribute to the flavour.

SERVES 4	250g (9 oz) basmati rice	2 x 2.5cm (1 inch) sticks of cinnamon
Preparation and cooking time: about 30 minutes	1/2 tsp yellow food colouring	4 cloves
	1/2 tsp red food colouring	2 bay leaves
	1 tbsp ghee (clarified butter, page 24) or olive oil	425ml (15 fl oz) cold water
	2 tsp finely chopped onion	1/2 tsp salt
	6 green cardamoms	

- Wash the rice in several changes of water and leave to drain in a large sieve.

- If using, mix each food colouring with about a tablespoonful of water, keeping the two colours separate, and set aside.

- Pre-heat the oven to 170°C, 325°F or gas mark 3.

- Meanwhile, heat the ghee or oil in a heavy-based pan with a tight-fitting lid, and fry the onion until just translucent.

- Add the cardamoms, cinnamon, cloves and bay leaves, and cook for 1 minute.

- Add the drained rice and mix well to coat all the grains with the ghee or oil. Cook on medium heat for about a minute.

- Stir in the water and salt, and bring to the boil. Once boiling, turn the heat to very low and place the lid on the pan.

- Stir the rice after about 5 minutes, and again after 3 minutes. Re-cover and leave for a further 4–5 minutes after which time all the water will have been absorbed.

- Add the food colourings to the rice, if using, by spooning in two separate lines across the rice for each colour.

- Replace the lid and put the pan in the oven for about 20 minutes to dry off the rice and set the colours.

- Transfer the pilau to a serving dish, taking care not to break the grains of rice. Fluff up with a fork. Serve immediately or cool as quickly as possible and refrigerate for use the next day.

- Re-heat in a microwave oven for about 2 minutes.

EGG FRIED RICE

This is quite a substantial dish to serve on its own, but is particularly so when combined with some pre-cooked vegetables or when eaten with a dhal.

SERVES 4	250g (9 oz) basmati rice	1 tsp salt
	6 green cardamoms	2 tbsp ghee (clarified butter, page 24) or olive oil
Preparation and cooking time: 30 minutes	2.5cm (1 inch) stick of cinnamon	2 tsp finely chopped onion
	4 cloves	2 eggs, lightly beaten
	2 bay leaves	2 tbsp soy sauce

■ Wash the rice in several changes of cold water and add to a large pan with the whole spices.

■ Add plenty of cold water so that the water is several centimetres (3 or 4 inches) above the rice and bring to the boil.

■ Stir in the salt and simmer for about 12 minutes or until the rice is cooked. Drain through a large sieve.

■ Place the sieve over a pan or bowl and leave the rice to drain completely. Remove the whole spices if preferred.

■ Meanwhile, heat half the ghee or oil in a heavy-based frying pan and fry the onion for about a minute.

■ Add the beaten egg and tilt the pan to spread the egg accross the base of the pan. Cook over medium heat for about 3 minutes until it is completely set.

■ Remove the omelette from the pan, roll up tightly and slice the roll thinly to obtain strips of omelette.

■ Heat the remaining ghee or oil in a karahi or large pan and add the drained rice. Stir-fry over medium heat for 4–5 minutes until heated through.

■ Sprinkle over the soy sauce and add the omelette pieces. Stir-fry for a further minute and serve.

Peshwari Pilau

The nuts and sultanas, lightly roasted in ghee, add a lovely crunch and sweetness to this rice dish. It is great with spicy curries.

SERVES 4	250g (9 oz) basmati rice	6 green cardamoms
	2 tbsp almonds, blanched	6 cloves
Preparation and cooking time: 30 minutes	2 tbsp pistachios	2 x 2.5cm (1 inch) sticks of cinnamon
	1 tbsp ghee (clarified butter, page 24) or olive oil	425ml (15 fl oz) cold water
	2 tbsp sultanas or golden raisins	1/2 tsp salt

■ Wash the rice in several changes of water and leave to drain in a large sieve. Chop the almonds and pistachios coarsely.

■ Pre-heat the oven to 170°C, 325°F or gas mark 3.

■ Heat the ghee or oil in a heavy-based pan with a tight-fitting lid and add the nuts, sultanas and whole spices. Cook gently for about 2 minutes, stirring.

■ Add the drained rice and mix well to coat all the grains with the ghee or oil. Cook on medium heat for about a minute.

■ Stir in the water and salt, and bring to the boil. Once boiling, turn the heat to very low and place the lid on the pan.

■ Stir the rice after about 5 minutes, and again after 3 minutes. Re-cover and leave for a further 4–5 minutes after which time all the water will have been absorbed.

■ Place the pan in the oven for about 20 minutes to dry off the rice.

■ Transfer the pilau to a serving dish, taking care not to break the grains of rice. Fluff up with a fork. Serve immediately or cool as quickly as possible and refrigerate for use the next day.

■ Re-heat in a microwave oven for about 2 minutes.

Saffron Pilau

Saffron is an expensive spice with a sweet, delicate aroma and deep auburn colour. It needs to be soaked in warm milk for a few minutes to release the colour and aroma. The resulting dish will be a pale yellow.

SERVES 4	1 tsp saffron strands	6 green cardamoms
	3 tbsp warm milk	2 bay leaves
Preparation and cooking time: 30 minutes	250g (9 oz) basmati rice	425ml (15 fl oz) cold water
	1 tbsp ghee (clarified butter, page 24) or olive oil	1/2 tsp salt
	2 tsp finely chopped onion	

- Combine the saffron and warm milk and set aside. Meanwhile, pre-heat the oven to 170°C, 325°F or gas mark 3.

- Wash the rice in several changes of water and leave to drain in a large sieve.

- Heat the ghee or oil in a heavy-based pan with a tight-fitting lid, and fry the onion until just translucent. Add the cardamoms and bay leaves, and cook for 1 minute.

- Add the drained rice and mix well to coat all the grains with the ghee or oil. Cook on medium heat for about a minute.

- Stir in the water, saffron mixture and salt, and bring to the boil. Once boiling, turn the heat to very low and place the lid on the pan.

- Stir the rice after about 5 minutes, and again after 3 minutes. Re-cover and leave for a further 4–5 minutes, after which time all the water will have been absorbed.

- Place the pan in the oven for about 20 minutes to dry off the rice.

- Transfer the pilau to a serving dish, taking care not to break the grains of rice. Fluff up with a fork. Serve immediately or cool as quickly as possible and refrigerate for use the next day.

- Re-heat in a microwave oven for about 2 minutes.

TIP

For a 'cheat's' version, use about 1/4 teaspoonful of turmeric instead of the saffron. Stir in with the water.

Mushroom Pilau

This mildly spicy rice dish with the meaty texture and taste of mushrooms is a delicious accompaniment to meat curries.

SERVES 4 Preparation and cooking time: 30 minutes	250g (9 oz) basmati rice 100g (3 oz) button mushrooms 1 tbsp ghee (clarified butter, page 24) or olive oil 2 tbsp finely chopped onion 6 green cardamoms 6 cloves	2 x 2.5cm (1 inch) sticks of cinnamon 2 bay leaves 1 tsp cracked black pepper 375ml (13 fl oz) cold water 1/2 tsp salt 1/2 tsp turmeric

■ Wash the rice in several changes of water and leave to drain in a large sieve. Pre-heat the oven to 170°C, 325°F or gas mark 3.

■ Wipe the mushrooms, trim the stalks and quarter. Heat the ghee or oil in a heavy-based pan with a tight-fitting lid and stir-fry the mushrooms for about 2 minutes until lightly browned.

■ Add the onion and all the spices and stir-fry for a further minute. Stir in the drained rice and mix well to coat all the grains with the ghee or oil. Cook on medium heat for about a minute.

■ Add the water, salt and turmeric and bring to the boil. Once boiling, turn the heat to very low and place the lid on the pan.

■ Stir the rice and mushrooms after about 5 minutes, and again after 3 minutes. Re-cover and leave for a further 4–5 minutes after which time all the water will have been absorbed.

■ Place the pan in the oven for about 20 minutes to dry off the rice.

■ Transfer the pilau to a serving dish, taking care not to break the grains of rice. Fluff up with a fork. Serve immediately or cool as quickly as possible and refrigerate for use the next day.

■ Re-heat in a microwave oven for about 2 minutes.

20. ACCOMPANIMENTS
CHUTNEYS, PICKLES AND RAITA

RELISH-LIKE condiments (*achaar*) and chutneys are embedded in Indian culture. In keeping with the richness and diversity of the cuisine, Indian pickles, chutneys and achaars, served with virtually every meal, come in a mind-boggling variety of types, flavours and colours. Mangoes, peaches, tomatoes, chillies, ginger, garlic, lemons, limes, carrots, aubergines, turnips, cauliflower, coriander, mint, coconut and many more fruits and vegetables are turned into pickles, chutneys or used in spicy yogurt dishes such as raita. Some preparations are as simple as grinding or mixing ingredients together, while others are complex, time-consuming concoctions of dozens of spicy and exotic ingredients, matured over months.

Indian chutneys and pickles are packed with fresh or pungent spicy flavours and are served in small quantities to whet the appetite and enhance the meal.

ACCOMPANIMENTS MENU

MANGO CHUTNEY
A sweet chutney made with ripe mangoes.

PEACH CHUTNEY
A sweet, fruity chutney made with ripe peaches and raisins.

COCONUT AND MINT CHUTNEY
A tart, spicy chutney made with coconut, fresh mint and spices.

LEMON PICKLE
A tart, salty pickle made with quartered lemons.

CRUNCHY PICKLED VEGETABLES
A spicy, vinegary salad of mixed shredded vegetables.

MANGO PICKLE
A salty pickle of tart green mangoes and whole spices in oil.

RAITA
A spiced, yet cooling yogurt dish with a variety of shredded vegetables.

MANGO CHUTNEY

Sweet mango chutney is a popular accompaniment to spicy dishes. Good quality mango chutney is quite expensive to buy so making your own not only saves you money; you will find it tastes much better too.

This chutney will keep well for up to two years so you can make a large quantity when mangoes are cheap and plentiful.

MAKES ABOUT 800ML (28 FL OZ)

Preparation and cooking time: 1hour 30 minutes

2kg (4 lb 8 oz) ripe mangos
500ml (18 fl oz/1 US pint) white wine or cider vinegar
350g (13 oz) white sugar
2 tsp grated ginger
2 red chillies, seeded and finely sliced (optional)

■ Peel the mangoes and discard the peel. Slice the flesh from the stones, chop coarsely and place in a large, heavy-based saucepan with all the remaining ingredients. Bring slowly to the boil, stirring to dissolve the sugar.

■ Simmer, partly covered, for 1 hour, stirring occasionally. Meanwhile, wash the jars and lids in hot soapy water, rinse well and dry in a warm oven.

■ Spoon the hot chutney carefully into the warm clean jars, place the lids on firmly and invert each jar for two minutes.

■ Store the chutney in a cool dry place. After opening, store in the fridge.

PEACH CHUTNEY

This sweet and sour, fruity chutney makes a nice change from mango chutney and goes well with cold meats, cheese and sausages as well as spicy curries. You can buy bruised and misshapen fruit but it's important that it is sweet and ripe as tasteless fruit will produce a poor quality chutney.

Ripe nectarines may be used instead of peaches.

MAKES ABOUT 500ML (18 FL OZ/ 1 US PINT) Preparation and cooking time: 2 hours	1 kg (2 lb 4 oz) ripe peaches 200g (7 oz) golden raisins 250ml (9 fl oz) cold water 2 large onions, sliced	370ml (13 fl oz) malt vinegar 250g (9 oz) white sugar 2 tsp grated ginger 1 tsp chilli powder

■ Wash the fruit well, remove the stones and chop the flesh coarsely. Place in a large, heavy-based saucepan with the raisins and water, bring to the boil and simmer, uncovered, for 20 minutes, stirring once or twice.

■ Add all the remaining ingredients and bring slowly back to the boil, stirring to dissolve the sugar.

■ Simmer, partly covered, for about 1 hour 15 minutes, stirring occasionally. Meanwhile, wash the jars and lids in hot soapy water, rinse well and dry in a warm oven.

■ Spoon the hot chutney carefully into the warm clean jars, place the lids on firmly and invert each jar for two minutes.

■ Store the chutney in a cool dry place. After opening, store in the fridge.

Coconut and Mint Chutney

This is a lovely fresh-tasting accompaniment to dhals (pulses) and curries and is also great in sandwiches. It keeps well in the fridge for up to five days.

MAKES ABOUT 250ML (9 FL OZ)

Preparation and cooking time: 15 minutes

1 bunch of mint (about 200g or 7 oz)
1 green chilli, roughly chopped
100g (3 oz) desiccated coconut
2 tbsp blanched almonds, roughly chopped

150ml (5 oz) plain yogurt
1 tsp salt
1/2 tsp garam masala

■ Remove the leaves from the mint and discard the stalks. Wash the leaves well and drain.

■ Place the mint leaves, chilli, coconut and almonds in the bowl of a food processor and process until finely chopped. Stir in the remaining ingredients and mix well.

■ Chill the chutney until required.

CRUNCHY PICKLED VEGETABLES

Another fresh-tasting accompaniment that goes well with most spicy dishes, this salad is simplicity itself to prepare. Choose any selection of crispy vegetables that are in season and full of flavour.

MAKES ABOUT 400ML (14 FL OZ)

Preparation time: 20 minutes

100ml (3 fl oz) cider vinegar or white vinegar
2 tsp sugar
1 tsp salt
1 tsp cracked black pepper
1/2 tsp cumin seeds

1 green chilli, finely chopped
1 carrot, julienned or grated
1 bunch of radishes, thinly sliced
1 red onion, thinly sliced
1/2 English cucumber, thinly sliced

■ Place the vinegar, sugar and salt into a large bowl and whisk until the sugar dissolves. Add the remaining ingredients and mix well.

■ Let the salad stand for about half an hour before serving to allow the flavours to develop.

MANGO PICKLE

If you like shop-bought mango pickle, you will love the home-made one. It is packed with so much more flavour that it will make your tastebuds tingle. It is quick and easy to prepare, but requires a little patience to let it mature before it is ready to eat.

Important note: It is essential that when preparing this pickle, your hands, all ingredients and containers are completely dry. No water must be allowed to seep into the pickle or it will go mouldy. You will need a large, clean glass or ceramic jar with a tight-fitting lid.

MAKES ABOUT 600ML (20 FL OZ)	6 medium or 8 small green mangoes	2 tbsp fennel seeds
	4 tbsp salt	2 tsp chilli powder
Preparation time: 20 minutes	50g (2 oz) mustard powder	150ml (5 fl oz) olive oil
	2 tbsp fenugreek seeds	150ml (5 fl oz) sesame oil

■ Rinse the mangoes and dry thoroughly. Place on a tray or large plate and air dry for at least 1 hour.

■ Slice the flesh along the stone, scraping off as much pulp as possible. Dice the flesh into bite-sized pieces and place in the jar along with all the bits of mango flesh. Sprinkle on the salt, place the lid on the jar and tighten. Shake the jar well and place on a sunny windowsill for a day.

■ Remove the lid and sprinkle the spices onto the mango in the jar. Pour on the oils, replace the lid tightly and shake the jar well to ensure everything is thoroughly combined.

■ Place the jar on a sunny windowsill, if possible for at least 7 days, shaking and mixing the ingredients daily.

TIP

If you don't have a sunny windowsill, salt the diced mangoes in a large microwave-proof bowl and microwave on high for 5 minutes, stirring the mangoes once half-way through. Allow to cool for 10 minutes, mix in all the remaining ingredients and transfer to a jar. Keep the jar in a warm place for several days, shaking it daily.

RAITA

Yogurt is a superb accompaniment to spicy foods and traditionally is served in some guise or another at every meal. It is a common side dish or accompaniment on the Indian restaurant menu as Raita, lightly spiced and usually combined with shredded cucumber. Cucumber is an excellent ingredient to use in Raita – it doesn't require cooking, is easy to prepare and has the right texture and mild flavour, but other vegetables or even fruits can be used to add variety.

I have used a combination of onion, cucumber and carrot but you might like to try grated daikon or radish, chopped tomato, shredded mint or finely diced melon or apple.

If you don't wish to make your own yogurt, purchase a good quality, preferably organic, commercial product.

SERVES 4		
Preparation time: 15 minutes	1/2 red onion, finely sliced 1 carrot, grated 1/2 cucumber, grated or julienned 1 small clove of garlic, finely chopped 1 green chilli, finely chopped 300ml (11 fl oz) yogurt (page 24)	1/2 tsp salt (or to taste) 1/2 tsp cumin seeds 1/2 tsp garam masala Pinch of turmeric (optional)

■ Combine all the ingredients in a large bowl and stir until well mixed. Refrigerate until required.

21. DESSERTS AND SWEETS

T HERE IS NO doubt that Indians are great lovers of spicy food. There is also no doubt that, somewhat paradoxically, a close second is their love for traditional Indian sweets or *mithai*. The consumption of mithai is more than a need to satisfy a sweet tooth, it is ingrained in Indian culture. Rich, expensive, luscious and gloriously sweet, lavishly decorated with sultanas, almonds, pistachios and silver leaf, mithai appears everywhere in Indian life. From birthdays to holy days, from religious ceremonies to wedding feasts, from simple gifts to lavish offerings, there is always a reason to give, receive and consume generous quantities of mithai. Indeed some occasions would simply not be complete without its presence.

Each region of India has its own specialities and there are hundreds of different variations of Indian sweets, but most are based on fresh, full-cream milk boiled down to make *khoa*, combined with ghee (clarified butter) and sugar in varying proportions. Other ingredients like besan (chickpea flour), carrots, pumpkin, rice and nut flours are used to create different types of sweets. Cardamom, cloves, mace, rose or *kewra* water are added to create exquisite flavours.

It was usual when I was growing up to make some of the less elaborate Indian sweets at home and there would always be a stash of *ladu*, *besan* or *barfi* to tuck into with a glass of milk on returning home from school, predictably made with pure ghee. Later I learnt to make *rasgulla*, the most popular modern-day sweet in India, *gulab jamon*, a regular on the restaurant sweet menu, *ras malai*, and the well known and loved Indian ice-cream, *kulfi*. No party, celebration or blessing ceremony was thinkable without a selection of these essential items.

Nowadays it is rare for Indian cooks to make any of these at home, with the exception of *kheer* (Indian rice pudding), which is a simple dish to make. Superb quality Indian sweets are available everywhere Indians have settled, and, although ghee is now rarely used, the end result has not suffered significantly.

Desserts and sweets menu

Kheer
A creamy rice and milk dessert made with basmati rice and fresh milk.

Cardamom Ice-cream
Home-made ice-cream flavoured with ground cardamom.

Mango Soufflé
A deliciously cool, light, fruity 'soufflé' made with ripe mangoes and cream.

Gajrella (Carrot Halwa)
Carrots, nuts and sugar combine to make this warming, luscious sweet.

Sweet Pullao
Basmati rice cooked in saffron-flavoured sugar syrup and flavoured with sweet, aromatic spices.

Kulfi
A quick recipe for an old favourite, using evaporated milk, sweetened and flavoured with cardamom and nuts.

KHEER

This rice 'pudding' is made with basmati rice, the grains of which have more aroma and a firmer texture than pudding rice, even after long, slow cooking. I like to make this sweet with 'lite' milk because I find the long, slow cooking makes the dish creamy enough, but you can use full fat milk if you prefer, for an even creamier dessert.

Kheer is delicious served warm or cold straight from the fridge.

SERVES 6–8

Preparation and cooking time: 2 hours

4 tbsp basmati rice
2 litres (70 fl oz/4.2 US pints) fat reduced or full fat milk
175g (6 oz) white granulated sugar

■ Wash the rice in a couple of changes of cold water and place in a large, heavy-based saucepan with the milk.

■ Slowly bring to the boil. Turn down the heat to very low, partly cover the pan, and simmer for about 1^1/$_2$ hours, stirring now and again. Add more milk if the mixture is too thick.

■ Stir in the sugar, and simmer for a further 20 minutes.

VARIATIONS:

Stir through a couple of tablespoonfuls of chopped almonds and pistachios, or a handful of sultanas about half-way through cooking.

Gajrella (Carrot Halwa)

The combination of grated carrots, nuts, cardamoms, sugar and pure ghee produces a sweet with a lovely texture and an absolutely delicious taste. Don't compromise on the ghee though; nothing else will do for this dessert.

Gajrella will keep in the fridge for several days, but halve the quantity of ingredients if you don't want to make so much.

SERVES 8–10

Preparation and cooking time: 1 hour

1 kg (2 lb 4 oz) carrots, grated
100g (3 oz) ghee (clarified butter, page 24)
1 tsp cardamom seeds, lightly crushed
100g (3 oz) almonds, blanched and chopped
100g (3 oz) pistachios, chopped
50g (2 oz) sultanas
125g (4 oz) caster sugar
125ml (5 fl oz) sweetened condensed milk
2 tbsp ground almonds

- Place the carrots in a large, heavy-based saucepan with 4 tablespoonfuls of water and cook, stirring, on high heat for about 3 minutes. Turn down the heat, cover and cook for a further 5 minutes, stirring once or twice.

- Add the ghee, turn up the heat again and stir-fry the carrots for a further 5 minutes.

- Lower the heat and stir in the cardamom and nuts, reserving about 2 tablespoonfuls. Continue to cook over low-medium heat, stirring frequently, until the carrots have turned a deep orange and the ghee starts to separate from them. This will take about 20 minutes.

- Stir in the sultanas and sugar and stir-fry on low heat for another 5 minutes. Add the condensed milk, turn up the heat a little and stir-fry the mixture for about 3 minutes.

- Stir in the ground almonds and mix over low heat until well combined.

- Serve warm, garnished with the remaining nuts, with thick cream or ice-cream. Or press into a Swiss roll tin, refrigerate until firm and cut into squares. Serve with tea or coffee.

Note: This recipe works best with organic carrots as they contain less water than their non-organic counterparts.

Sweet Pullao

A dish that celebrates the versatility of rice beautifully, this sweet, perfumed pilau is simple yet quite exquisite.

The typical beautiful deep-yellow colour of this sweet is unfortunately as a result of artificial food colouring, but you can leave it out and have a dish that is paler in colour but still tastes wonderful.

SERVES 6–8	
Preparation and cooking time: 30 minutes	1 tsp saffron 2 tbsp warm water 220g (8 oz) basmati rice 1 litre (35 fl oz/2.1 US pints) hot water 175g (6 oz) granulated sugar 1/4 tsp yellow food colouring (optional)	60g (2 oz) ghee (clarified butter, page 24) 6 cardamoms 6 cloves 2 tbsp almonds, blanched 100g (3 oz) sultanas

■ Combine the saffron and warm water, and set aside. Wash the rice in several changes of water and leave to drain for several minutes.

■ Meanwhile, put the hot water and sugar in a large saucepan, and place over low heat, stirring to dissolve the sugar. Once the sugar has dissolved, turn up the heat and bring to the boil. Turn off the heat and stir in the colouring if using.

■ Heat the ghee in a large, heavy-based saucepan and add the rice. Stir until the grains of rice are well coated with the ghee.

■ Add the cardamoms, cloves, almonds and sultanas. Stir-fry for 2 minutes.

■ Carefully (as it will spit) pour in the sugar syrup. Turn the heat down to very low, stir in the saffron water, and simmer gently for about 30 minutes, stirring now and again to ensure the rice cooks evenly.

■ Turn off the heat and let the rice stand, covered for 10 minutes. Fluff up with a fork and serve hot or cold.

KULFI

Often referred to as Indian ice-cream, kulfi is still one of the most popular sweets on the Indian restaurant menu. This quick recipe cuts out a lot of time-consuming effort but still produces a wonderful result.

SERVES 6	300ml (11 fl oz) light evaporated milk	1/2 tsp ground cardamom
Preparation time: 20 minutes (plus time for freezing)	4 tbsp caster sugar 100ml (3 fl oz) thick cream 15g (1/2 oz) almonds, blanched and finely chopped	15g (1/2 oz) pistachios, finely chopped 1 tbsp chopped pistachios to serve

■ Heat half the milk in a small pan, add the sugar and stir to dissolve over low heat. Cool.

■ Place all the remaining ingredients except the nuts in a large bowl, add the sweetened milk and whisk until well combined.

■ Stir in the nuts and divide the mixture among 6 kulfi moulds. Freeze until completely hardened.

■ Dip the moulds in hot water to loosen the frozen kulfi and serve sprinkled with more nuts if desired.

TIP

If you don't have kulfi moulds, freeze the mixture in shallow trays, remove from the freezer about 15 minutes before serving, and cut into squares.

Index

Also available in *Right Way*:

The original bestseller

THE CURRY SECRET
HOW TO COOK REAL INDIAN RESTAURANT MEALS AT HOME

Kris Dhillon's curry classic now updated with new recipes for more mouthwatering curries.

Some praise from readers:

'Truly an excellent book and one that any Indian restaurant fan who enjoys cooking should have.'

'The Holy Grail of curry cook books.'

'This book is so good it's unbelievable.'

Also available:

CHINESE COOKERY SECRETS
HOW TO COOK CHINESE RESTAURANT FOOD AT HOME

Deh-Ta Hsiung shares his life-long knowledge of Chinese *restaurant* cooking to help you successfully reproduce your favourite meals at home – from a simple, single dish to an elaborate grand feast. He shows you each crucial stage of preparation to enable you to recreate the harmonious blending of subtle flavours, delicate textures, aromas, colours and shapes that are the hallmarks of authentic Chinese cooking.

To order these Right Way titles please fill in the form below

No. of copies	Title	Price	Total
	The Curry Secret	£5.99	
	Chinese Cookery Secrets	£5.99	
	Slow Cooking Properly Explained	£4.99	
	For P&P add £2.50 for the first book, £1 for each additional book		
	Grand Total		£

Name:

Address: Postcode:

Daytime Tel. No./Email (in case of query):

Three ways to pay:

- Telephone the TBS order line on 01206 255 800. Order lines are open Monday – Friday, 8:30am – 5:30pm.

- I enclose a cheque made payable to TBS Ltd for £

- Please charge my   [ ] Visa   [ ] Mastercard   [ ] Amex   [ ] Maestro (issue no   )

Card number:

Expiry date: Last three digits on back of card:

Signature: (your signature is essential when paying by credit or debit card)

Please return forms to Cash Sales/Direct Mail Dept., The Book Service, Colchester Road, Frating Green, Colchester CO7 7DW.
Enquiries to readers@constablerobinson.com.

Constable and Robinson Ltd (directly or via its agents) may mail, email or phone you about promotions or products.

[ ] Tick box if you do not want these from us   [ ] or our subsidiaries.

www.right-way.co.uk
www.constablerobinson.com